THE LACE WARS

ARMS and UNIFORMS

Other titles in this series:

Arms and Uniforms 1 – *Ancient Egypt to the 18th Century*

Arms and Uniforms 2 – *18th Century to the Present Day*

The Napoleonic Wars 1

The Napoleonic Wars 2

The First World War 1

The First World War 2

The Second World War 1

The Second World War 2

The Second World War 3

The Second World War 4

The Lace Wars 2

THE LACE WARS

PART I

France – The King's Household and the Infantry under Louis XV and Louis XVI; The British and Prussian Infantry from 1700 to 1800

Liliane and Fred Funcken

WARD LOCK LIMITED . LONDON

Contents

First published in Great Britain in 1977 by Ward Lock Limited, 116 Baker Street, London W1M 2BB, a member of the Pentos Group.

House editor Gill Upton
Text filmset in Baskerville
by Servis Filmsetting Ltd, Manchester

Printed and bound in Belgium by
Casterman S.A. Tournai

British Library Cataloguing in Publication Data

Funcken, Liliane
The lace wars.
Vol. 1: France—the King's Household and the Infantry under Louis XV and Louis XVI; the British and Prussian Infantry from 1700 to 1800.—
(Arms and uniforms).
1. Uniforms, Military—History 2. Arms and armor—History
I. Title II. Lucas, Jean III. Funcken, Fred
IV. Series
355. 1'4'094 UC485.E/

ISBN 0-7063-5562-7

Foreword

The discovery, twenty years ago, of plates of illustrations arranged like a chess-board from the enormous work by Doctor Lienhart and René Humbert *The Uniforms of the French Army from 1690 to the present day* (1895) gave us a real surprise.

Noticing our obvious interest, the Curator of the Engravings Room of the Royal Military Museum in Brussels produced more surprises, amongst them the four hundred plates of romantic illustrations by Noirmont and Marbot (1830–60) and the no less famous work by Mouillard, *The French Regiment under Louis XIV (1887)*. This volume and its sequel are based on these three monumental works which have become rare and command prices generally considered prohibitive.

We have had to modify these illustrations and to restore the colours which had faded due to their original sparing application. This was because their use had made the original editions, printed in lithography, so costly.

These few improvements are in no way intended as a correction to the originals. Rather, our work should be considered a homage to the memory of the great masters, the pioneers in the study of uniform who opened the way for so many artists and researchers and who are, so often, the target of the inevitable 'authorities' who invariably allude only to the few errors of detail.

The hundreds of uniforms depicted in this book, especially those of the first half of the eighteenth century must be considered only as sketchy reproductions drawn from descriptions, often incomplete, found in contemporary texts.

The subsequent work of early twentieth-century artists such as Benigni, Hilpert, Job and Toussaint, the German R. Knötel in his colossal *Uniformkunde* containing nearly two thousand plates, the Austrian Ottenfeld and the Englishman Simkin have been valuable guides for us, as was one of the military painters of our day, Eugène Leliepvre.

Should the reader's curiosity be further aroused by this book he might like to refer to the illustrations in the admirable series of *L'Armée Française* by Lucien Rousselot which will furnish innumerable details.

The fine, but alas too short, series of illustrations by Colonel MacCarthy are well researched and attractive, and a superb work on the same theme. Finally, specialized pamphlets, particularly from collectors' societies, have benefited not only from the above mentioned masters, but also from specialist studies and are consequently very authoritative.

We would like once more to express our gratitude to Monsieur Lorette, curator of the Museum of Engravings and Monsieur Leconte, chief curator of the Military Museum in Brussels thanks to whose active and kindly interest we have had access to very rare documentation.

Our thanks also to Mr W. Y. Carman, honorary curator of the Imperial War Museum in London, for his invaluable advice.

Liliane and Fred Funcken

FRANCE – THE KING'S HOUSEHOLD

In 1445 Charles VII of France acquired a hundred Scottish archers to act as his personal guard, and so formed the basis of the first royal military household. However, it was not until the seventeenth century that both the civil and military branches of the household were completely established.

The palace militia was divided into: the Guard responsible for the internal security of the Louvre, composed of the Bodyguard (les gardes du corps), the Swiss Hundreds (les cents-suisses), the Guards of the Door and the Provost Guards; the Guard responsible for the surroundings of the Louvre; the Gendarmes; the Light Horse (les chevau-légers); the Musketeers; and the Mounted Grenadiers.

Since the King's Household had a reputation for unconditional bravery and devotion to the service of its monarch, the command of these companies was highly contested by noblemen throughout the kingdom.

The regiments of French and Swiss guards are the ones usually associated with the King's Household, however, we shall also include in this section, the Gendarmerie. It was not actually part of the household, but had, by tradition, the privilege of marching in front of the cavalry, and so deserves to be included as do their predecessors, the Maréchaussée. These first chapters, about the soldiers in what is known as 'The Lace Wars', will be concluded with a section on the princes' household.

FRANCE—THE KING'S HOUSEHOLD
BODYGUARDS I

1. Standard-bearer of the 1st Scottish Company in 1721. In the 1st French Company the basic colour for the standard, the shoulder belt and the decoration of the saddle was blue; in the 2nd French Company it was green and in the 3rd it was yellow—2. Officer of the Scottish company in 1721—3. Guard of the 3rd company in 1721—4. Guard of the 2nd company in 1721—5. Guard of the 3rd company in 1745—6. Detail of the standard.

1
2
3
4
5
6
L. & F. Funcken

The Bodyguard

Around 1423 or 1428, the first company of bodyguards or body archers, composed of 125 wild Scotsmen, was mustered and became known as the 'Scottish' company. Subsequently, a second and third company were created by Louis XI, both of them French.

The fourth company was formed in the reign of Francis I on 27 March 1515. At that time, each of these four companies was composed of only a hundred men.

A statute of 1664 outlawed the mercenary status of the bodyguards and they thus became an exception at the very centre of the army. This measure did not, however, prevent the cost of this corps rising to the exorbitant sum of 80,000 livres.

The members of this force were certainly very comfortably off and their numbers had reached 1,600 during the reign of the 'Sun King', Louis XIV. In 1715 on the accession of Louis XV, their strength was reduced to 1,440.

A statute of 6 January 1737 limited each company's strength to six brigades of fifty-five each, forming two squadrons of 165 guards, including twelve brigadiers, twelve lance-corporals, six standard-bearers, six trumpeters and one kettle drummer. The total strength of the four companies was 1,320 horsemen.

A literary work of 1761 tells us that each company was composed of 336 men, divided into two squadrons of 168 or into six brigades of fifty-six commanded by a captain – more often than not a duke. A census of 1762 shows that the bodyguards comprised four companies of 367 men formed into eight squads, a total of 1,468 men. This magnificent corps survived until 12 September 1791.

To join, one had to be at least 1.6m (5ft 4in) in height, well built and 'full-faced', of mature age, of noble family or at least 'above average' and of course, belong to the Roman Catholic church.

On 6 October 1789 a member of these bodyguards made a last desperate stand against the riotous crowd invading the Queen's bedchamber. His name was Varicourt and his last cry before he was literally cut to pieces was 'Save the Queen!'

FRANCE—THE KING'S HOUSEHOLD BODYGUARDS II

1. Trumpeter in 1724—2. Kettle drummer in 1724—3. Trumpeter in 1786—4. Officer of the 3rd company in 1786—5. 2nd company in 1786—6. 4th company in undress uniform in 1786.

1
2
3
4
5
6
L. & F. FUNCKEN

The Guards of the Sleeve and The Scottish Guards

From the core of the Scottish Company of bodyguards (*see above*) twenty-four gentlemen selected from among the longest serving members were recruited. Father Gabriel Daniel, author of the *History of France* (1713) and the *History of the French Militia* (1721) has explained that the title 'Garde de la Manche' or 'Guard of the Sleeve' stemmed from the fact that during Mass a guard, armed with a halberd, stood on either side of the king. The clothing worn on this occasion was a tabard, or tunic, embroidered with a coat of arms on a white background worn over the bodyguard's uniform.

Two Guards of the Sleeve were always at the king's side, one on his right and the other on his left. In addition, on the death of the monarch, they had the privilege of guarding his body without wearing mourning, placing him in the coffin and then putting the sarcophagus into the tomb.

For special ceremonies such as the coronation or the marriage of the King, six of the longest serving Guards of the Sleeve wore a special uniform made of white satin with a coat of arms embroidered in gold. They were known as Scottish Guards and their captain had the title of 'First Man-at-Arms of France'.

The old Scottish company from which these guards were drawn had been commanded by Scottish lords of the highest distinction since the fifteenth century. Subsequently, they had even more illustrious leaders, including James VI, son of Mary Stuart in 1584, his son Henry under Henry IV, followed by his brother Charles I and finally the Duke of York, the future James II.

Since the reign of Francis I, the force had ceased to be purely Scottish. Gradually the Scottish company of the bodyguard became Scottish in name only and was recruited from French troops. However, they retained the custom of replying 'Hamir' to the call of the watch. This was traditionally a corruption of the English 'I am here'.

FRANCE—THE KING'S HOUSEHOLD
GUARD OF THE SLEEVE AND
SCOTTISH GUARD

1. Guard of the Sleeve in 1724—2. Scottish Guard in 1724—3. Guard of the Sleeve in 1786. The national cockade which appears at the bottom of the tunic is just one of the features of this extraordinary ostentatious costume—4. Herald at arms in 1786.

1
2
3
4
L. & F. FUNCKEN

The Swiss Hundreds

The origins of the Company of the 'Swiss Hundreds' goes back to the first five hundred Swiss introduced into France by John of Anjou, the Duc de Calabre, at the beginning of the war for Public Good fought in 1464 against King Louis XI. The latter, realizing the value of these mercenaries, took six thousand of them into his army in 1478. It was not, however, until the reign of Charles VIII that the first company of the Swiss Hundreds was formed, with Louis de Menton as its first colonel-in-chief. At this time (1496) it comprised one hundred men plus twenty-seven officers of all ranks.

The Swiss Hundreds were entrusted with service in the palace along with the bodyguard. Their particular role was as 'Guard on the Doors' of the royal apartments.

During ceremonies, they surrounded the royal coach and their captain, who wore an extremely elaborate costume for ceremonial occasions, would always walk in front of the sovereign.

For most occasions, the Swiss Hundreds were armed with a halberd and dressed in the rich blue and red clothing of the King's livery. However, in 1771, they started to wear a campaign uniform which was more suitable for military exercises and it is in their 'Spanish Dress' that these soldiers are most familiar.

Henri Bouchot, in his *Eulogy of French Military Dress*, beautifully illustrated by Job, described these soldiers as 'unutterable lackeys'. Even if one accepts this judgement, one must not be too harsh on the thousands of Swiss soldiers who served France so loyally for four centuries.

It is interesting to notice that the mercenary system was actively opposed by the Swiss authorities from the fifteenth century onwards and, at this time they formed the 'Foreign Service' which gave young men an opportunity to better themselves and to escape from the humdrum way of life of an over-populated country.

The treaties of alliance signed with the great powers, contained 'military clauses' which allowed the 'Helvetian Corp' to provide troops in exchange for important commercial advantages.

FRANCE—THE KING'S HOUSEHOLD
THE SWISS HUNDREDS

1. Officer in 1724—2. Captain in ceremonial dress in 1724—3. Guard in 1724—4. Drummer wearing ceremonial dress in 1786—5. Guard wearing ceremonial dress in 1786—6. Guard in full dress in 1786—7. Officer in full dress in 1786—8. Guard in campaign dress in 1771—9. Flag used from the middle of the eighteenth century to 1791. It is not known when the motto was added.

EA
EST
FIDVCIA
GENTIS
9
1
2
3
4
5
6
7
8
L. & F. FUNCKEN

Guards of the Door and the Provost

Guards of the Door

Considered by some historians to be the oldest royal guard, this fifty-strong company guarded the inside doors of the Palace from six in the morning, handing over at six in the evening to one of the corporals of the Scottish Guard.

In 1663, there were on the roll, one captain, called the sentry captain, four lieutenants and fifty guards.

Besides a salary of two hundred livres, each guard received several annual gratuities, up to one hundred and seventy-two livres. In addition, they were given ten crowns from the offertory treasurer each time the King laid hands on those suffering from Scrofula.[1]

The company was disbanded by Louis XVI on 30 September 1787.

The Provost

The Provost Guards of the King's Mansion were under the orders of the Provost of the Palace, or the Provost Marshal of France who had the rank of captain. These guards were in charge of the police and the execution of the law at court and at any place the sovereign might be.

When the King rode in his coach the Provost Guards preceded the Swiss who marched directly in front of the royal vehicle. Their tunic was decorated with a club similar to that of Hercules and the motto *Erit haec quoque cognita monstris* (This club will also be known by monsters).

In 1778 the company was reorganized and the numbers fell from one hundred to sixty, and then rose to sixty-eight two years later. They were apparently disbanded in 1787 at the same time as the Guards of the Door.

[1] The kings of France were believed to have the power of curing scrofula (a kind of abscess). They used to touch the sufferers especially after the coronation ceremony. This custom was continued until 1825 in the reign of Charles X.

FRANCE—THE KING'S HOUSEHOLD
GUARDS OF THE DOOR AND THE PROVOST

1. Provost Guard in 1724—2. Officer of the Provost Guards in 1724—3. Officer of the Guards of the Door in 1724—4. Guard of the Door in 1724—5. Provost Guard in undress uniform in 1786. Stockings were red and shoes had copper buckles—6. Guard of the 2nd company of Provost Guards in 1786—7. Uniform of the Guards of the Door and detail of the drum—8. Partizan of a sergeant of the Guards of the Door—9. Uniform of the Guards of the Door. Non-commissioned officers wore an identical one except for the shoulder belt. Breeches and stockings were red, and the garter and ribbon around the hat, silver. The general form was the same as for fig 6—10. Belt buckle. All these details apply to the uniform of 1786.

7
8
9
10
5
6
2
3
1
4

The Gendarmes of the Guard

The Gendarmes, established in 1609 by Henry IV to guard the Dauphin were retained by Louis XIII and according to a statute of 1667, came immediately after the bodyguards in order of precedence. They had a higher status than the Light Horse regiment, from which they differed very little, because of a surviving feudal tradition which valued knights who were armoured from head to toe more than lightly-armed horsemen.

This corps of gendarmes acquired more privileges than any other corps in the King's Household. Its four senior officers had the right to sell the position of gendarme, but this practice was abolished in 1664.

Under Louis XIV the company numbered as many as 250 men but in 1697 it was reduced to its original number of 200. It remained unchanged under Louis XV and was abolished on 30 September 1787.

With the King as their captain, the gendarmes had the special honour of accompanying the standards into the King's bedroom right up to his bedside. The same curious ceremony was carried out, but in reverse order, when the monarch decided to review his troops or to leave for the country.

During the eighteenth century, the corps had a General Staff composed of a first lieutenant, three second lieutenants, three ensigns and three flag-bearers. The corps also included a disciplinary commissioner, ten sergeants, eight corporals, eight lance-corporals, four standard-bearers, four staff officers, four trumpeters and one drummer.

The senior officers rode grey horses whilst the rest of the company rode bays.

FRANCE—THE KING'S HOUSEHOLD
GENDARMES OF THE GUARD

1. Gendarme in 1724—2. Officer in 1724—3. Lance-corporal in 1724—4. Drummer in 1724—5. Gendarme in 1786—6. Trumpeter in 1786—7. Drummer in 1786—8. Officer in 1786—9. Gendarme in 1786—10. Standard from 1602 to 1787. The reverse was grey with the usual scattering of golden fleurs-de-lis.

1
2
3
4
5
6
7
8
9
10

The Light Horse Regiment of the Guard

The Light Horse originated as the personal company of the future Henry IV who was indebted to his friend the Seigneur de la Curée for this excellent troop.

In its proper form the company of the Light Horse Regiment of the Guard had a strength of a hundred men and was granted its privileges on 15 December 1593. It replaced the two companies of a hundred gentlemen nicknamed 'crowbeaks' who had, up till then, been in charge of guarding the Sovereign. This nickname came from the war-hammer whose head vaguely resembled a crow's beak.

From then on Henry IV made this company his ordinary mounted guard and became its captain himself. The company numbered successively 120 men (including officers) in 1611, 200 in 1627, 182 in 1640 and was once more increased to 200 men by Louis XIV in 1669.

Under Louis XV it comprised a first lieutenant, two second lieutenants, four cornets,[1] ten sergeants, two staff officers, eight corporals, four standard-bearers,[2] four assistant staff officers, four trumpeters, a drummer and two hundred light horsemen. In addition, there was a certain number of officers for the 'use of the corps' such as the almoner, apothecary, veterinary surgeon etc.

The commoner who managed to buy a position in the Light Horse was made a nobleman after five years' service but the great lords very quickly took over supervision of the enrolments.

The almost total destruction of the company at the battle of Dettingen and the loss of face against the Austrians and the Anglo-Hanoverians in 1743 gave its commander M. de Chaulnes an excuse for asking the King to forbid the enrolment of any subjects from families with less than two hundred years of 'nobility'.

Expensive to run and showing very little real worth in time of war, the company was severely attacked by Louis XVI's War Minister who wanted to disband it. It took all the influence of the Duc d'Aiguillon, its commander, to delay this move, but a royal statute of 18 January 1776 reduced the Light Horse to twenty-three officers and second officers and forty men. They were finally disbanded on 30 September 1787.

[1] The Cornet was a junior lieutenant who carried the unfurled standard at one of the extremities or 'horns' (*cornes*) of the company.

[2] The standard-bearer was a non-commissioned officer who carried the standard rolled up in its cover.

FRANCE—THE KING'S HOUSEHOLD
LIGHT HORSE GUARD

1. Light Horse Guard in 1724—2. Corporal in 1724—3. Light Horse Guard in undress campaign uniform in 1745—4. Officer in 1745—5. Trumpeter in 1786—6. Light Horse Guard in 1786—7. The last uniform worn before the disbandment on 30 September 1787—8. Detail of the gold lacing as usually reproduced in great classical works—9. Real appearance from contemporary drawings (1756) by Eisen—10. Standard of the Light Horse (1580 to 1787) with the motto *Sensere Gigante* (Giants have felt this). The reverse showed a scattering of fleurs-de-lis on the same grey silk background. The fringes were of gold and silver.

8
9
1
5
3
2
6
7
4
10
L. & F. FUNCKEN

The Musketeers of the Guard

This famous company of horsemen was formed in 1662 during the reign of Louis XIII.

The first company of musketeers was formed by equipping a company of carabiniers with muskets. Louis XIII made himself captain and appointed the famous M. de Troisvilles or de Tréville to command it under his orders, along with a first lieutenant, a second lieutenant, an ensign, a sergeant and two corporals.

The musketeers served both as infantry and cavalry, accompanying the King on his journeys but never entering his apartments. It was for this reason that they always wore wide-topped boots, whereas the bodyguards wore high-heeled shoes for their daily duties.

This company was disbanded in 1646[1] and was reformed in 1657 when it had 150 men, a first lieutenant, a second lieutenant, a cornet player, an ensign and two sergeants.

Meanwhile, a similar company had been formed to guard first Richelieu and then later, Mazarin. When the latter died in 1660 this company was adopted by the King's household with the title of 2nd Company of Musketeers. It did not take up its duties with the monarch until 1663 and served only as infantry.

Disbanded in 1664, it was immediately reorganized along the same lines as the first company. From January 1665 King Louis XIV became its captain[2] probably in recognition of its service during the Lorraine expedition of 1663.

In 1663, each company comprised 300 musketeers, but this number was reduced to 250 in 1668. These figures did not include the forty-four officers and non-commissioned officers, the six drummers, the four oboe players, the apothecary,

[1] This was due to the hatred of Mazarin, who, on the King's death, took his revenge on the troublesome guards. He only reformed them in order to put his nephew, Philippe, Duc de Nevers, in charge.

[2] The King was also captain of the 1st company.

FRANCE—THE KING'S HOUSEHOLD
MUSKETEERS I

1. Musketeer of the 2nd company in 1729—2. *Idem* in 1724—3. Standard-bearer of the 2nd company in 1724—4. Corporal of the 1st company in 1724—5. Officer of the 1st company in 1724—6. First lieutenant of the 1st company in 1724—7. Standard of the 1st company, 1657 to 1776. It was fringed with gold and silver. The reverse side was dotted with golden fleurs-de-lis—8. Standard of the 2nd company, 1657 to 1776 with the same reverse side as the preceding one.

1
2
3
7
8
4
5
6
L. & F. Funcken

the nine surgeons and others who swelled the numbers of each of the two companies. Their numbers were greatly increased in time of war by volunteer noblemen.

When serving as infantry, the musketeers carried a flag, and had drums and pipes, but, when on horseback, they had standards and trumpets. By 1663, only the drummers remained, then mounted. Mounted oboe players had replaced the pipers and the trumpeters.

The grey or white horses of the 1st Company and the black of the 2nd explain the names 'grey musketeers' and 'black musketeers' by which they were known. The origin of the nickname 'Great musketeers' by which the members of the 1st company were designated is more mysterious. It probably refers to the difference in origin of the two companies and reflects the old rivalry which existed between the King's guards and those of the Cardinal. There is also another name in contemporary texts, common to both companies, that of 'The King's Red Household'. It comes from the musketeers' coat and trousers of scarlet cloth, which they provided at their own expense. The king provided the cloak and sleeveless surcoat which were characteristic of their corps.

The musketeers were extremely proud of their rigorous discipline, their nobility, their uniform and, of course, their great courage. In 1667 at Valenciennes, they gained the admiration of the whole army by leading the assault like ordinary infantrymen. During the eighteenth century they distinguished themselves at the siege of Philippsburg[1] in 1734, at Fontenoy[2] in 1745 and at Cassel[3] in 1766.

The Duke of Burgundy, the Dauphin (heir to the throne) was a musketeer but to avoid any jealousy, he belonged to both companies and wore their uniforms alternately.

[1] On a tributary of the Rhine, to the north of Karlsruhe. Site of many battles in the course of the seventeenth and eighteenth centuries.

[2] In Belgium, 7km to the south-east of Tournai. A victory for the Marshal de Saxe at the head of the French over the English and the Dutch, during the war of Austrian Succession.

[3] Or Kassel, a town in west Germany (*Hesse*) occupied by the French in the middle of the eighteenth century (the Seven Years' War).

The reform of the King's Household between 1775 and 1776 forced Louis XVI to abolish these two fine troops in order to save money. They were reassembled in 1789 but disbanded soon after by the Republic.

FRANCE—THE KING'S HOUSEHOLD MUSKETEERS II

1. Oboe player of the 2nd company in 1730—2. Drummer of the 1st company in 1730—3. Drummer of the 1st company in 1730. He is wearing the same full sleeves as in fig 2. Note also the light boots or *gamaches* worn mainly by the dragoons. As the expert Eugène Leliepvre has pointed out, the musketeers were the dragoons of the King's Household and it is therefore quite likely that they would have worn this type of footwear—4. Musketeer of the 1st company in 1744—5. Musketeer of the 2nd company in 1772.

1
2
3
4
5
L. & F. Funcken

The Horse Grenadiers

This company was formed by Louis XIV in December 1676. The Horse or Mounted Grenadiers were armed with muskets, a pistol and a sword and carried digging implements to clear the way for the other troops of the King's Household at whose head they marched.

At first, the corps numbered a first lieutenant, two lieutenants, two second lieutenants, two sergeant-majors, four sergeants, two corporals, four lance-corporals and seventy-four grenadiers; the captain was the King himself. The officers all belonged to the nobility but the instructors were chosen from among the foot grenadiers. All were tall and had moustaches.

In 1678 the company totalled 120 men, a number which was reduced a year later to a hundred after the Peace of Nijmegen.

In 1725 the numbers were further reduced to eighty-four men but by an order of 1759 they recruited 150 grenadiers from the Corps of Grenadiers of France.[1]

The Horse Grenadiers were abolished on 15 December 1775 and its members dispersed to different regiments with the rank of N.C.O.

This select troop, famous for its manoeuvres and arms drill, covered itself with glory in the year following its creation, at Valenciennes, Cambrai and Charleroi. The Horse Grenadiers also took part in the difficult and bloody campaigns of 1702 to 1706, notably at Ramillies. They appeared again at Oudenaarde in 1708 and in 1709 at Malplaquet.[2] Their last campaign was that of 1761 during the Seven Years' War, but they had taken part in many other campaigns notably at Fontenoy in 1745.

They certainly lived up to the motto embroidered on their standard which they received at the glorious battle of Leuze[3] in 1691 – *Undique terror, undique lethum* (everywhere terror, everywhere death).

[1] The Corp of the Grenadiers of France had been formed from the companies of grenadiers taken from 48 reformed regiments on 15 February 1749

[2] See page 94 in the chapter on Marlborough.

[3] Between Tournai and Ath in Belgium. A victory for the Marshal of Luxembourg nicknamed 'The Wallpaperer of Notre-Dame' because of the number of flags he captured from the enemy and hung in the cathedral.

FRANCE—THE KING'S HOUSEHOLD
HORSE GRENADIERS

1. Grenadier, 1690 to 1720. After 1720 the pistol on the right was replaced for a time by a tool, a pick or an axe, hung with the iron part at the top, in a black leather case—2. Drummer in 1721. The drum casing was decorated with flaming grenades—3. Officer in 1721—4. Grenadier, 1735 to 1756—5. Grenadier in 1774. Taken from a water-colour of the time—6. Detail of the headdress. Note that according to certain contemporary artists such as Eisen and Parrocel, the hat was sometimes worn with the point towards the front (see fig 4).

TERROR UNDIQUE
UNDIQUE
LETHUM
1
2
3
4
5
6
7
L. & F. FUNCKEN

The French Guards

Their Origins

Pierre de Bourdeilles, who lived from 1540 to 1614, gives the date as 1563 for the founding of the French Guards. In his diary he wrote 'with Le Havre captured and the English once more expelled from France, the King, and the Queen his mother, who held all the power because of her son's minority, formed a French Watch Regiment of foot soldiers to guard His Majesty. This was therefore the first institution composed of ten ensigns of the King's Guard.' Catherine de Medicis persuaded her son Charles x to distribute the new regiment between several garrisons.

A few months later the Huguenots tried to seize the King on the road from Meaux to Paris. The dispersed guards were immediately re-united and ordered to keep a close watch over the King.

In 1573 after the capture of La Rochelle, Charles IX felt that his enemies, the Huguenots, were so weakened that he could safely do without his guards. However, the Protestant unrest in the following months and the threat of more fighting again forced the King to have a bodyguard, although it was now reduced to three companies instead of the original ten.

Charles' successor, Henry III who had given up his claim to the throne of Poland to become King of France, soon re-established the regiment on its original footing.

Organization

From 1574 onwards the number of French guards increased: fourteen companies in 1591, twenty in 1596 and thirty in 1635. Louis XIV added two companies of grenadiers in 1689 and his successor added a third in 1719 to make a total of thirty-three companies.

The strength of these companies was not always the same. At first, the regiment had fifty men in each company; in 1600 there were eighty, in 1615

FRANCE, REGIMENT OF THE SWISS AND FRENCH GUARDS I

1. Piper of the Swiss Guard—2. Drummer of the French Guard—3. Guard—4. Officer—5. Guard.

1
2
3
4
5
L. & F. FUNCKEN

there were two hundred and in 1629, three hundred.

During the reign of the Sun King (Louis XIV) the number was once more settled at three hundred. This meant that the total force of the regiment, after the creation of the two new companies, reached 9,600 men.

This number was reduced to 4,100 by Louis XV and fixed by his successor at 4,878 men distributed in the following manner:

According to an order of 17 July 1777 the regiment had six battalions each, composed of four companies of fusiliers and one company of grenadiers.

A company of fusiliers had a captain, two lieutenants, an ensign, a sergeant-major, a regimental sergeant-major, four sergeants, a quartermaster clerk, an officer standard-bearer, an officer-gunner, nine corporals, three gunners, a surgeon, 144 fusiliers, and four drummers – 176 men in all.

The grenadier company comprised a captain, a vice-captain, two lieutenants, two second lieutenants, a sergeant-major, a regimental sergeant-major, four sergeants, a quartermaster clerk, eight corporals, a surgeon, eighty-four grenadiers, and three drummers – a total of 109 men.

Each company also accepted two supernumerary cadets.

Privileges

The French Guard Regiment had, in every respect, an advantage over the other corps, even the Swiss Guard.

During a campaign, the regiment had the right to choose its fighting position and it usually put itself in the centre of the first line of infantry. During a siege they were always placed ahead of the trenches ready to leap through any breach which the sappers could make.

The French Guards also had first choice of quarters in the garrisons. All the officers of the regiment were mess companions of the King and enjoyed the right of 'committimus' which allowed them to plead at the Court of Petitions, in Parliament or before any other special tribunal. Non-commissioned officers, for their part could only be judged by their peers. The sergeants, after being accepted by the colonel had to appear in front of a

FRANCE, FRENCH GUARDS II

1. Officer in undress uniform in 1757—2. Officer in dress uniform in 1757—3. Adjutant in 1786—4. Officer in undress uniform in 1786—5. Officer in dress uniform in 1786—6. Orderly sergeant in 1786.

6
1
2
5
4
3
L.&F. FUNCKEN

'Chamber of Admission'. This was made up of inexperienced sergeants from the regiment who examined the candidate and had the final word on whether or not he could be promoted.

The French Guards had the honoured privilege of leading the troops when they marched into any place which surrendered after a siege.

Under the Revolution

Foreigners were not allowed into the French Guards who recruited some of their men from Paris and were generally popular there. They served as policemen at markets and in the towns and were nicknamed 'Pierrots', a pet name for sparrows. When the Revolution started these troops were among the first to support the movement. Their connection with Paris had meant that they were well used to the 'new ideas'.

At Versailles they were responsible for guarding the Royal Family and as 'Outside Guards' they placed a sentry on the right of the door, opposite the Swiss Guard on the left.

When the Revolution came the entire regiment supported it, for there had been growing dissatisfaction over a number of points. Thiers wrote in his *History of the French Revolution* 'An opportunity to air their grievances soon presented itself. The French Guards, the elite troop designed to be the King's guard were in Paris.[1] Four companies would leave there in turn to serve at Versailles. The new discipline was very severe and the men were also unhappy about their new colonel. Soldiers and junior officers felt that all chance of promotion was closed to them; they were hurt and upset at seeing the young officers doing hardly any duty, appearing only on review days and not even accompanying the regiment to the barracks. Indiscipline was rife and a few soldiers were imprisoned in the Abbaye.[2] Everyone gathered at the Palais Royal shouting "To the Abbaye". The crowd immediately followed. The doors were broken down and the soldiers who had just been seized were led out in triumph. (30 June 1789).' A deputation from Parliament presented itself later

[1] At the Courtille Barracks, Faubourg du Temple.

[2] Former prison of the Abbey of Saint-Germain-des Prés where the September massacres of 1792 took place.

FRANCE, FRENCH GUARDS III

1. Guard in 1757 and a variation of the collar—2. Guard in 1785—3. Flag-bearer in 1785—4. Drummer in 1785—5. Sergeant of the Grenadiers in 1787—6. Grenadier in 1787—7. Detail of the back of the fur bonnet.

1
2
3
4
5
6
7
L. & F. FUNCKEN

to Louis XVI and easily obtained the pardon and favour of the King.

The next year, on 12 July, the French Guards had an opportunity to show their gratitude to the people of Paris. In the Place Vendôme,[1] a group of demonstrators had been charged by a regiment of the Royal German Cavalry. Injured people were left lying on the ground, amongst them a soldier from the French Guards. Some of his friends, billeted in the Place Louis XV,[2] had had a brawl with members of the Royal German Cavalry and so they immediately opened fire and drove back the aggressors towards the Tuileries. Unfortunately, the peaceful crowd already there, was brutally dispersed by the Prince de Lambesc and his men. An innocent old man was killed in the confusion and this skirmish was to spark off the general revolt which led to the storming of the Bastille two days later.

The French Guards were, of course, on the scene and cooly managed to save thirty-two Swiss Guardsmen and eighty-two disabled people from the fury of the crowd. Two guards, Elie and Hullin tried desperately, but in vain, to save De Launay, the governor of the Bastille, from a terrible end.

On 31 August 1789 this famous regiment was disbanded but was immediately absorbed into the citizen's miltia which later became the National Guard under the command of La Fayette. In October 1792 when troops were urgently needed at the front, the National Guardsmen dispersed to other regiments forming the main officer material for the new revolutionary army.

[1] Place Vendôme should have been called 'Place des Conquêtes'; in fact, it was called 'Louis-le-Grand' from 1699 to the Revolution, 'Place des Piques' from 1793 to 1799 and 'Internationale' in 1871 under the Commune.

[2] Soon to be 'Place de la Révolution', and later (1795) 'Place de la Concorde'.

FRANCE, FRENCH GUARDS IV

1 and 2. Negro cymbal players in dress and undress uniform in 1786—3. Drum major in 1786—4 and 5. Drummers in dress and undress uniform—6 and 7. Musicians in undress and dress uniform. Note the clarinet case down the right thigh of fig 7. The instrument in fig 6 is a bassoon.

1
2
3
4
5
6
7

The Swiss Guards

Origins

The true Swiss Guards date from 1616 and a precise date is given in the *Memoirs* of François de Bassompière, Colonel-in-Chief of the Swiss and Grisons Guards in 1614: 'Louis XIII, on his return from Guyenne, where he was married, decided to form, in Tours, a complete regiment of Swiss Guards and they arrived to stand in front of his residence, on Tuesday 12 March.'

Most of the twelve companies of the new regiment comprised three officers, a captain, a lieutenant and an ensign but a few had two captains, each of whom commanded half the company.

Louis XVI thought this number was insufficient and ordered five officers to be appointed to each company with eight sergeants, four pikemen, in the personal service of the captain, six corporals and six *ampessades*.[1] Each company had a piper and five drummers.

Organization

On 1 June 1763 a statute reorganized the regiment in the following fashion: a general company which should march at the head of all the others, eleven companies of fusiliers and, for the first time, four companies of grenadiers, each forming four battalions and four companies.

The main company staff was composed of a judge (the company had its own court), an almoner, a secretary-interpreter, a doctor, a surgeon with the rank of major, a sergeant, a quartermaster, a provost, sixteen musicians and an ensign with the rank of second lieutenant. Its ordinary staff was the same as the other companies of fusiliers: a captain, two lieutenants, two second

[1] '*Ampessade*' comes from the Italian '*lancia spezzata*' (broken lance) from the fact that this elite soldier, recruited from the nobility, shortened his lance to serve in the infantry. All the following forms are to be found: lancespezates, lancespezzates, lancepessade, lance passade, lancepecat, lanspessade, lanspassade and anspessade.

FRANCE, SWISS GUARDS I

1. Non-commissioned officer in 1721—2. Officer in 1721—3. Guard in 1721. He is standing in the regulation attitude (under arms). Certain sources say the decoration on the pouch is silver—4. Officer in 1757—5. Guard in 1750.

1
2
3
4
5
L. & F. FUNCKEN

lieutenants, six sergeants, two quartermasters, twelve corporals, twelve salaried clerks and a drummer for 132 ordinary soldiers.

Each company of grenadiers comprised: a captain, two lieutenants, two sergeants, a quartermaster, four corporals, four salaried clerks and a drummer plus forty grenadiers.

At first, the Swiss guard companies were billeted in the outskirts of Paris and in the neighbouring villages such as Courbevoie, Rueil or Neuilly. Later, in the reign of Louis XV, a magnificent barracks was built.

Recruitment and Privileges

Apart from the main company which accepted men from all of the thirteen Swiss cantons, each company of the Swiss Guard was recruited from a different canton.

There was complete freedom of religion. They were paid twice as much as the French troops but because of very precise agreements (see page 14) France could not employ these 'contracted soldiers' against Germany, Spain or Italy outside the French frontiers as these nations also used soldiers from the 'Helvetian Corps'.

The Supreme Sacrifice

The Swiss Guards were recalled to Paris shortly before that fatal day 10 August 1792. This was an unfortunate decision as their devotion to the royal family was well known and the crowds detested them.

A young lawyer's clerk Philippe Morice lived through the drama at the Tuileries palace: 'While both parties were hurling abuse at each other, a few of the more daring patriots came forward . . . they attacked two Swiss sentries with hooked pikes. . . . The Swiss on duty joined battle at the orders of captains Zusler and Castelberg . . . and fired on the assailants who had just set upon two of their comrades. The noise of the firing was the signal for general fighting. . . . The Swiss were the only ones to hold firm but being attacked from both the courtyard and the garden, and having already lost many of their colleagues, two hundred of these brave soldiers withdrew and regrouped under the colonnade . . . they continued to fire, using up all their cartridges; they all perished. . . . In a few minutes the crowd rushed through the apartments like a flood, killing all the Swiss they could find. They cut the throats of any unfortunate guards found lurking in corners and alcoves. Others were thrown, alive, through the windows, begging in vain for their lives but they were simply run through with pikes.'

Loyal unto death the Swiss guards sacrificed themselves to defend an empty palace!

FRANCE, SWISS GUARD II

1. Standard-bearer with the regimental flag. The colours, in the form of flickering flames, were typical of the Swiss regiments (see the special section on flags)—2. Corporal of the Fusiliers. In the reign of Louis XVI the corporals and the sergeants of the Swiss regiments carried a baton called a *schlague* (from the German *schlagen*—to knock) which became purely decorative. When armed, this object was worn hanging by its cord from a buttonhole with the end tucked into the fold of the uniform as shown in fig 7—3. Grenadier officer—4. Higher ranking officer—5. Musician—6. Sapper—7. Sergeant of the Grenadiers—8. Drummer.

1
2
3
4
5
6
7
8
L. & F. Funcken

The Gendarmerie of France

This Gendarmerie, also called the 'Gendarmerie of the King and Princes', originated when the bands of heavily armed cavalry – or men of arms (gens d'armes) – and the lightly armed soldiers, called the 'Light Horse' regiment joined forces. They then became the Gendarmerie of France.

The first statute reorganizing this fine company appeared in 1665. It was ranked second to the King's Household and so marched at the head of all the cavalry of the line.

Noblemen, officers unable to maintain a company themselves but anxious for a military career, old and respected soldiers who had been instructors in the cavalry and had so been granted a title, were all acceptable. Thus, those who had gained their titles through military exploits, noblemen by birth and commoners all met within its ranks.

In 1720 the thirty-three companies of the ancient peace-keeping force, the Maréchaussée were made part of the Gendarmerie. The Comte de Saint-Germain[1] tried, about forty years later, to give the corps a uniform constitution by uniting it with the cavalry. The Marquis de Castries who was its commander actively opposed the idea.

In 1763, Choiseul finally reformed the Gendarmerie by uniting it with the companies of the Light Horse cavalry disbanded on the 5th June. The ten companies thus formed were grouped in three brigades representing a total of 1,500 gendarmes.

[1] This is not the famous adventurer, but his namesake, later to become Secretary of State for War and instigator of many reforms.

[2] They belonged originally (in 1686) to the military household of the Grand Dauphin, son of Louis XIV.

In 1772, the ten companies were:

1. Scottish gendarmes
2. English gendarmes
3. Gendarmes from Burgundy
4. Gendarmes from Flanders
5. Queen's gendarmes
6. Dauphin's gendarmes[2]
7. Gendarmes from Berry
8. Gendarmes from Provence
9. Gendarmes from Artois
10. Gendarmes from Orléans

Only eight companies remained by 1775 after the suppression of the Provence and Orléans companies.

The corps was dissolved between 1787 and 1789. It is in no way the ancestor of the present *Gendarmerie Nationale* – despite many statements to the contrary.

FRANCE, THE FRENCH GENDARMERIE

1. The colours of the English 'Gendarmes' in 1724. The standard was usually carried in its support fixed to the right stirrup—2. Ensign of the Scottish Gendarmes in 1724—3. Trumpeter of the Orléans company in 1724—4. Kettle drummer of the Burgundy company in 1724—5. Commissioned officer of the Burgundy company in 1767—6. Officer of the Queen's company in 1757—7. Gendarme of the Berry Regiment in 1776.

Uniforms from 1737 to 1764: 8. Scottish Gendarmes—9. English Gendarmes—10. Burgundy Gendarmes—11. Flanders Gendarmes—12. Brittany Gendarmes.

Uniforms from 1764 to 1775: 13. Scottish Gendarmes—14. English Gendarmes—15. Burgundy Gendarmes—16. Flanders Gendarmes—17. Queen's Gendarmes—18. Brittany Gendarmes.

Special emblems: 19. Orléans company—20. Queen's company—21. Anjou company.

8
9
10
11
2
12
1
13
3
20
19
14
21
4
15
5
7
16
17
18
6
L. & F. FUNCKEN

The Maréchaussée of France

These were the true predecessors of the gendarmes, dating back to a much earlier era than the '*gens d'armes*' who became the 'Gendarmes of France', dealt with in the last section.

The Maréchaussée was run for a long time as separate units in the provinces and was only organized nationally in the reign of Louis xv by an edict dated 16 March 1720. At that time there were thirty-three companies.

The first of these was called the company of the High Constable[1] and was the 'Chief Company'. This company was responsible for the security of the Constable's residence and the archives. They were also on duty inside the court itself, where the Marshals of France settled points of honour between noblemen and soldiers. The implementation of their verdicts was assured by the guards who would 'garrison' the house of the accused and later take him to prison.

The ordinary officers of the High Constable Regiment, not including the Marshals, had to be acquainted with every lawsuit or dispute between men of arms, war commissioners and superintendents, army suppliers, etc. These officers were represented in the Army by a 'Provost General of the Constabulary and Maréchaussée of France'.

Company of the Provost General of the Mint

This corps, formed in 1635 was not given military standing until the reign of Louis xv who entrusted it with the secruity of the Mint.

The company comprised thirty-three officers and second officers, forty-four guards and a trumpeter.

[1] The High Constable (the most famous of whom was du Guesclin), was a high official of the Crown who had his own court, the *Connétablie*. The office of Constable was abolished by Richelieu but the Constable's court and its company of marshals continued under the authority of the marshals of France.

Company of the Provost General of the Maréchaussée of the Ile-de-France

Placed under the control of the Secretary of State this company was responsible for policing the outskirts of Paris. Its strength was fifteen officers and adjutants (exempts),[2] forty-four horsemen and two trumpeters.

[2] Exempt: In certain companies of Guards, the officer who took charge in the absence of the captain and lieutenants was exempt from ordinary duties. The custom of choosing an officer from the lower ranks of the Maréchaussée to be the 'exempt' meant that this title became the usual one for the leader of a squad in the Maréchaussée.

FRANCE, GENDARMERIE AND MARÉCHAUSÉE

1. Guard of the Maréchaussée in 1724—2. Guard of the High Constable, Provost General in 1724—3. Guard of the Provost General of the Maréchaussée of the Ile-de-France in 1724—4. Guard of the company of the Provost General of the Mint in 1724—5. Guard of the High Constable in 1724—6. Horseman of the Maréchaussée in 1786.

Standards of the Gendarmerie of France forming part of the King's Household: 7. King's Scottish Gendarmes, 1622 to 1788—a. English Gendarmes—b. Dauphin's Gendarmes—c. Brittany Gendarmes—d. Anjou Gendarmes—e. Berry Gendarmes—f. Orléans Gendarmes—8. Burgundy Gendarmes—9. Flanders Gendarmes—10. Queen's Gendarmes. All the standards had the reverse side decorated with fleurs-de-lis on a background of the same colour as the right side. As regards example 7, the mottoes changed as in the following list:

TUUS/AD TE NOS VOCAT/ARDOR—Your ardour calls us to you
IN/PERICULA/LUDUS—There is sport in danger
TRIUM/PHALI STIPITE/SURGIT—It rises from a glorious stock
VIRTU/TEM AUCTHORE/REFERT—It brings virtue to the user
VESTI/GIA MAGNA SE/QUETUR—It will follow great footsteps
ALTER/POST FULMINA/TERROR—There will be another terror after the thunderbolt.

7
OMNI MODO
IN
8
9
PLURIBUS
NEC
IMPAR
SUB SIDERE
PRISCI
PATRUM
10
PACEM SEU BELLA
SEU
GERO
c
d
e
f
1
2
3
4
5
6

Regular Companies of the Maréchaussée

These thirty companies were distributed around the provinces, their strength depending on the population of the area to be policed. This corps totalled 2,850 horsemen including thirty provost generals, 104 lieutenents and 164 'exempts' (see page 42). On 27 December 1769 a statute increased the number of brigades in the Maréchaussée to 200. Three years later a special company was formed 'for the king's hunts' but in the same year, 1772, the corp was reduced by 1,000 men and totalled only 3,500 gendarmes. In 1780 the strength was raised to 4,609 men but in 1791 the Maréchaussée of France, split up by the decrees of 18 August and 22 September 1790, were replaced by the *Gendarmerie Nationale* with *Valeur et Discipline* as its motto.

The Princes' Household

Monsieur's[1] Guard

Formed by Louis XV on 1 April 1771, this corp comprised two companies. Each one included a captain, a lieutenant, a deputy lieutenant, three second lieutenants, a sergeant-major, two corporals, two lance-corporals, forty guards and one trumpeter.

The 1st company had golden yellow as its distinctive colour and the 2nd had purple. They were abolished in 1792.

Guards of the Comte d'Artois[2]

Their formation on 17 November 1773 only took effect in March 1774.

The two companies were of more or less the same strength as Monsieur's guards but with an additional two second lieutenants and ten guards in each company.

[1] Brother of Louis XVI, the future Louis XVIII. The title of 'Monsieur' was given to the younger brother of the king.

[2] Other brother of Louis XVI, the future Charles X.

The staff of each of these two corps had: a major, two standard-bearers, a war commissioner, a surgeon with the rank of major, a treasurer, an almoner, a clerk of the watch and a kettle drummer.

Princes' Swiss Bodyguard

These were formed at the same time as the other troops in the Princes' military household.

The corps was composed of a first lieutenant, a sergeant-major, two ensigns, four exempts, two quartermasters, an almoner, a commissioner, a secretary, a treasurer, two corporals, twenty-eight guards and a drummer.

They were abolished in 1792.

The Princes' Guards of the Door

Formed in 1772 they comprised: the colonel, two lieutenants, a sergeant-major and twenty-five guards. They were disbanded in 1788.

FRANCE, THE PRINCES' HOUSEHOLD, 1786

1. Monsieur's Swiss guard—2. The Comte d'Artois' Swiss guard—3. The Comte d'Artois' guard of the door—4. Monsieur's guard of the door—5. Monsieur's bodyguard from the 2nd company—6. Comte d'Artois' bodyguard from the 1st company.

1
2
3
4
5
6
L. & F.
Funcken

The Staff

The Army Staff was largely composed of the General Staff, aides-de-camp and the regimental officers, plus the staff corps.

The General Staff

The General Staff included Marshals of France and Generals. The usual insignia of the Marshals of France was the famous baton which was covered in royal blue velvet and decorated with golden fleurs-de-lis embroidered in relief.

It was only towards 1724 that the marshals and generals had a real uniform with easily recognizable features. This uniform underwent very few changes between this time and the Revolution.

The generals were divided into two categories: lieutenant-generals and camp marshals or *maistres de camp généraux*, ranks which correspond to the Division Generals and Brigade Generals of today.

The rank of Marshal entailed different duties at different periods of history. It replaced the rank of brigadier abolished in 1788.

In the reign of Louis XIV camp marshals were so numerous and they squabbled so often over precedence that the rank of General Camp Marshal had to be created to keep order amongst them. The Camp Marshal's duties gradually became so indefinite that eventually they merged in with those of the Marshals of France.

The Staff Corps

This corps, formed in 1665, only began to operate effectively in 1783. An elite of officers was placed at the disposal of the generals during a campaign. It was abolished in 1790.

The Aides-de-Camp

During the last three reigns before the Revolution the aides-de-camp on the staff of each general officer were as follows:
for a marshal: one colonel, one lieutenant-colonel and two captains; for a lieutenant-general: two captains; for a camp marshal: one captain.

Flags

The custom of nailing a piece of cloth to the staff of a lance goes back to the fifteenth century. The term *drapeau* was adopted for the first time in 1583 but it was not then a word in general use.

The White Flag

The White Flag, originally a scarf, became a personal ensign, a distinctive mark of the rank Colonel General and it was they who introduced and maintained this practical display of their authority. The colonels of some provincial regiments were keen to copy this practice as a way of showing their independence and authority. Louis XIV, jealous of the growing influence of these Colonel Generals forbade this office, keeping it only for himself. The famous white flag therefore became, if not the national, at least the royal flag.

The Colonel's Flag

For a long time the ancient 'drapeau colonelle' or company flag, was carried only by six regiments nicknamed the 'old corps' or the 'old bands': The French Guards, those of Picardy, Champagne, Piedmont, Navarre and Normandy. Later in 1635 it became the 'old-timers' flag and was carried by the Richelieu, Bourbonnais, Auvergne, Talard and Pons regiments and the King's regiment.[1] Gradually it was granted to the more recently formed regiments. By 1661 nearly all regiments had been given the right to carry flags and they were the responsibility of specially chosen soldiers from the oldest companies.

This emblem varied enormously from one corp to another. More often than not it took the form of the regimental flag, in white on white and decorated with the colonel's coat of arms or his motif or motto. It was first officially called the colonel's flag or *drapeau colonel* in 1753.

The Regimental Flag

This famous insignia, slashed by the white cross of the Armagnacs who supported the French in the Hundred Years' War, has been reproduced in numerous illustrations. It remained almost unchanged up to the Revolution.

The Infantry flags originally measured 2.10 × 2.28m under Louis XIV, 1.78 × 1.78m in 1725 (according to Rigo) and 1.54 × 1.62m at the end of Louis XVI's reign.

In 1703 each battalion had three flags, in 1749 only two and finally one only in 1776. There were only a few regiments which did not follow this rule and they were nearly all foreign.

To avoid mistakes which, in the heat of battle might lead soldiers to confuse friend and foe, a white bow was adopted after the battle of Fleurus[2] in 1690. This was tied under the iron bar, on the staff, with a cord in the colours of the flag, decorated with fringed tassels.

Despite this measure the vast number of colours caused such confusion that it provoked this comment in the 'Encyclopédie': 'Plant flags in the middle of a plain and ask the soldiers if they know under which flag they must rally'.[3]

[1] The *petits vieux* or 'old timers' had the right, in case of disbandment, to remain in the younger corp called *bâtards* (bastards).

[2] In Belgium, to the north-east of Charleroi. A victory for the Marshal of Luxembourg (see page 26, note 3). It was the site of other famous battles in 1794 and 1815.

[3] *Encyclopédie ou Dictionnaire raisonné des sciences, des arts et des métiers* by Diderot. 17 volumes of writing and 11 volumes of illustrations edited between 1751 and 1772.

The Infantry of the Line

The first uniforms hardly differed from civilian dress having enormous cuffs, wide tails and the roomy jacket that was then fashionable. The fact that all the soldiers in each regiment dressed alike made this dress into a uniform. These civilian clothes were gradually changed and modified to take on a military appearance.

The first, and by far the most important change was to make the cuffs in very vividly coloured cloth. As this distinctive colour alone was insufficient to distinguish one regiment from another, they had the idea of sewing differing numbers of buttons onto the cuffs. They also varied the size and position of the pockets as well as the number of buttons that fastened them. The decoration of these pockets was peculiar to each regiment and served to distinguish one from another thus giving a sense of identity to the troops.

In the first years of the eighteenth century the French foot soldier was dressed in a greatcoat made of the cheapest off-white cloth, cut like the jacket.

From 1697 onwards a standard type of hat was adopted. It was edged with gold or silver braid and decorated with a black cockade.

The Regulations[1]

The first known regulation was made in March 1729, but it was just a number of directives which, as Rigo[2] said, recommended that cloth from Lodève and serge from Aumale should be used to make military coats.

[1] Regulations concerning uniform and the organization of the army.

[2] Albert Rigondaud, known as 'Rigo', painter of the French Army and creator of a remarkable series of illustrations called *Le Plumet* showing First Empire uniforms and flags of the old regime.

FRANCE, GENERAL STAFF

1. Officer of the Infantry in 1724—2. Marshal of France in 1724. He is wearing a polished breastplate under his uniform —3. Camp Marshal in 1767—4. Aide-de-Camp in 1767—5. Lieutenant General wearing full dress in 1786—6. Camp Marshal wearing undress uniform in 1786—7. Staff officer in 1786—8. Army Commissariat.

FRANCE, REGIMENTAL FLAGS (pages 50 and 51)

1. Picardy, 1569 to 1791—2. Champagne 1569 to 1791—3. Navarre, 1589 to the middle of the eighteenth century—4. Piedmont, 1569 to 1791—5. Normandy, 1616 to 1791—6. The Navy, 1636 to 1791—7. Bourbonnais, 1584 to 1791—8. Rohan-Soubise—9. Auvergne, 1636 to 1791—10. Flanders, 1763 to 1791—11. Guyenne, 1763 to 1791—12. The King's, 1770 to 1791—13. Royal, 1663 to 1791—14. Poitou, 1682 to 1791—15. Lyonnais—16. Dauphin, middle of the eighteenth century to 1791—17. Gondrin—18. Touraine, 1657 to 1791 —19. Anjou, 1776 to 1791—20. D'Eu, previously Maine—21. Dauphiné, 1762 to 1791—22. Montmorin—23. Souvré—24. Queen's—25. Limousin, 1684 to 1791—26. Royal Vessels, 1649 to 1791—27. Orléans, 1660 to 1791—28. La Couronne, 1673 to 1791—29. Brittany—30. Du Perche, 1775 to 1791—31. Artois, 1673 to 1771—32. Berry, 1763 to 1791—33. Hainaut, 1763 to 1791—34. La Sarre, 1686 to 1791—35. La Fère, 1651 to 1750—36. Alsace (German regiment), 1656 to 1791—37. Royal Roussillon, 1667 to 1791—38. Condé, 1659 to 1791—39. Bourbon, 1667 to 1791—40. Beauvaisis, 1685 to 1791—41. Rouergue, 1671 to 1791—42. Burgundy—43. Royal Navy, 1669 to 1791—44. Vermandois, 1669 to 1791—45. Saxe (German regiment)—46. Royal Artillery—47. Royal Italian, 1671 to 1791—48. Bettens (Swiss regiment)—49. Seedorff (Swiss regiment)—50. Monin (Swiss regiment) —51. Vigier (Swiss regiment)—52. Languedoc, 1672 to 1791—53. Puyguyon, 1705 to 1791—54. Wittemer (Swiss regiment)—55. Médoc, 1691 to 1711—56. Vivarais, 1763 to 1791—57. Chaillou—58. Royal Comtois—59. Monconseil—60. Provence, 1675 to 1780.

L. & F. Funcken
1
2
3
4
5
6
7
8

1
2
3
4
5
7
8
9
10
12
PAR
DECORI
VIRTUS
13
14
15
17
18
19
20
RES
PRESTANT
NON VERBA
FIDEM
22
23
24
25
27
28
DEDIT
HANC
MASTREKA
CORO
NAM
29
POTIVS
MORI
QUAM
FÆDARI
30

32 33 34 35
37 38 39 40
42 43 44 45
47 48 49 50
Auxilium Nostrum
a Dom ino
52 53 54 55
57 58 59 60

1736

As a result of the experiences in the War of Polish Succession which had broken out three years earlier, the Secretary of State for War corrected a few obvious faults in the clothing and also took a new step towards a more clearly defined system of uniform. The order issued on 20 April 1736 was much more detailed than the preceding one. Listed below are the essential points, for to detail the entire text or even that of the valuable *Abrégés* by Lemau de la Jaisse[1] would be unnecessary. The illustrations and captions emphasize the most interesting aspects.

The coat or jerkin was no longer to be buttoned to the belt. The cuffs were to be 'en botte', that is, with a seam and not open at the bottom, as before. Buttonholes down the back were abolished, as were coloured jackets and breeches (though this ruling was rarely observed). Coloured lapels were seen for the first time. When they reached down as far as the waist they were called 'bavaroises'. The front panels of the coat were turned back and were called 'retroussés'.

1757

Turned back collars in the same colour as the cuffs were introduced and coloured lapels became more common. These lapels could be fastened up to the top with hooks in the winter and the coat was also fastened with four buttons across the stomach.

The cuffs, nearly all of them 'en botte' were smaller. Heart-shaped pieces began to appear on the folded part to reinforce the hooks.

1762

Admiration for Prussian military styles led to the adoption of a completely new white uniform by nearly all the French regiments. The exceptions were the first six regiments who had a white one trimmed with blue and the 7th and 9th regiments who had an off-white one. The cuffs were nevertheless the same width as the sleeves and the lapels had a varying number of buttons. These details, plus the appearance of additional distinctive regimental colours, made it easier to distinguish between the regiments. Each regiment wore its number which denoted its rank and seniority, thus putting an end to the perpetual squabbles between officers of different regiments over precedence.

1767

The turned back collar was replaced by a band of white or coloured cloth. The number of buttons on each lapel was fixed at seven while the four buttons under the right lapel were reduced to three.

From 1767 to 1775 innumerable new styles of head-gear appeared; hats big and small, with three or four corners, helmets made of copper or dressed leather in the shape of a truncated cone, or else the dragoon type with a plume. The latter was worn by the soldiers from 1771 to 1775 and by the Colonel General Regiment until 1791.

[1] A series of seven works entitled *Abrégés de la carte militaire de France sur terre et sur mer*, published between 1734 and 1741. They were the sequel to the *Carte générale de la Monarchie et du militaire ancien et moderne*, published in 1733.

FRANCE, 1720–1736 I
CIRCA 1720

The numbering of the sketches gives both the regiment and its position of rank in the list of corps. For example: Number 1 = First regiment, number 2 = Second regiment etc.

1. Picardy—2. Navarre—3. Champagne—4. Piedmont—4a. Officers of the Piedmont Regiment—5. Normandy—6. The Navy—6a. Officers of the Navy—7. Bourbonnais—8. Richelieu—9. Auvergne—10. Tallard—11. Pons—12. King's—12a. Officers of the King's regiment—13. Royal—14. Poitou—15. Lyonnais—16. Dauphin—17. Gondrin—18. Touraine—19. Anjou—20. Du Maine—21. Noailles—22. Choiseul—23. Souvré—24. Queen's—25. Limousin—26. Royal Vessels—27. Orléans—28. La Couronne—29. Brittany—30. Du Perche—31. Artois—32. Rochechouart—33. D'Ouroy—34. La Sarre—35. La Fère—36. Alsace—37. Royal Roussillon—38. Condé—39. Bourbon—40. Beauvaisis—41. Rouergue—42. Burgundy—43. Royal Marine—44. Vermandois—45. Saxe—The 46th regiment, part of the Artillery, is not shown here—47. Royal Italian—48. May—49. Brendlé—50. Bettens—51. Burky—52. Languedoc—53. Puygyon—54. Médoc—55. Duras—56. Senneterre—57. Royal Comtois—58. Monconseil—59. Provence—60. Mortemart—61. Wittemer—62. Bezenval—63. Mailly—64. Nice—65. Toulouse—66. Guyenne—67. Lorraine—68. Flanders—69. Berry—70. Béarn—71. Hainaut—72. Boulonnais—73. Angoumois—74. Périgord—75. Saintonge—76. Bigorre—77. Forez—78. Tournaisis—79. Cambrésis—80. Foix—81. Bresse—82. La Marche—83. Quercy—84. Nivernais—85. Brie—86. Soissonnais—87. Ile-de-France—88. Vexin.

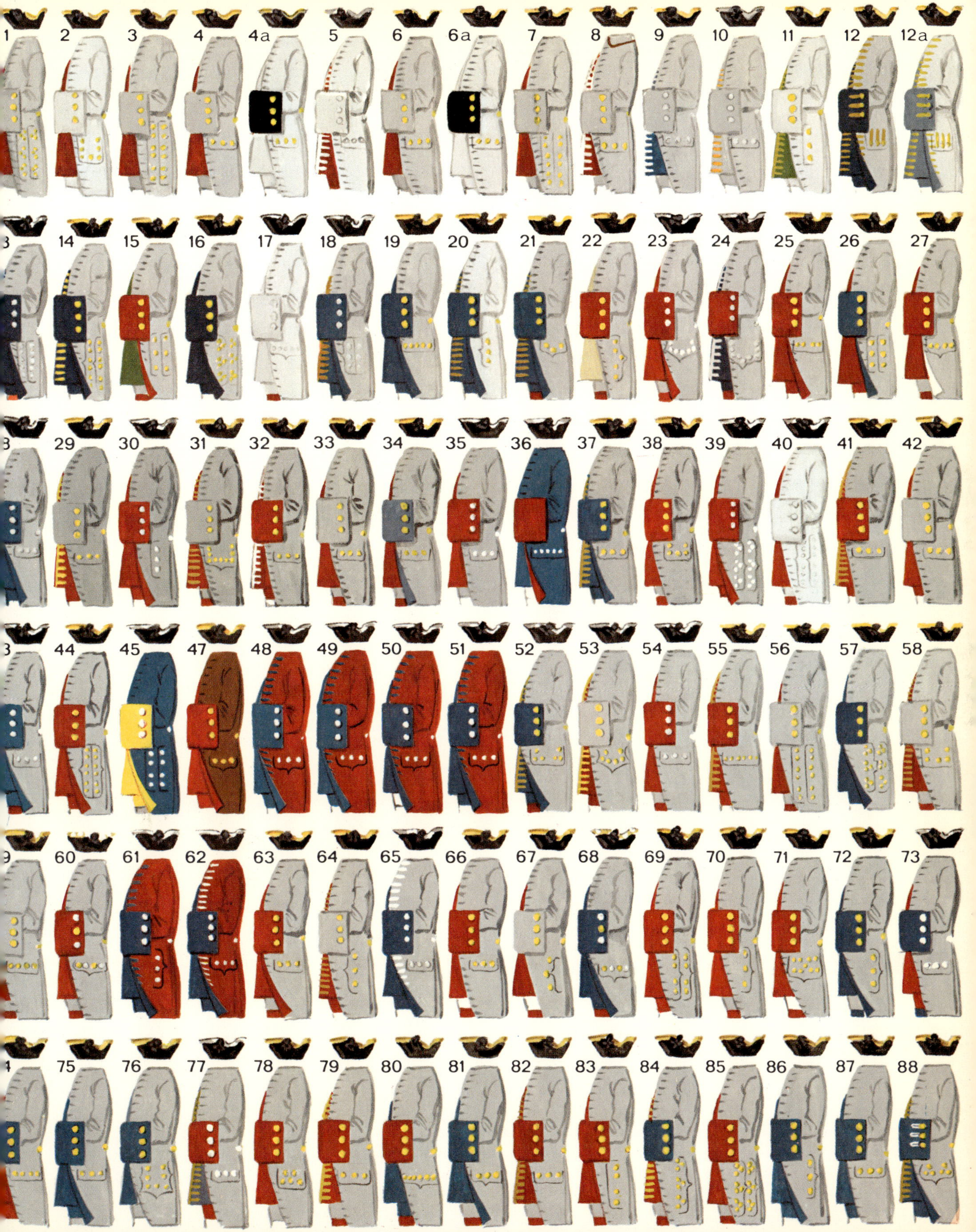
1
2
3
4
4a
5
6
6a
7
8
9
10
11
12
12a
14
15
16
17
18
19
20
21
22
23
24
25
26
27
29
30
31
32
33
34
35
36
37
38
39
40
41
42
44
45
47
48
49
50
51
52
53
54
55
56
57
58
60
61
62
63
64
65
66
67
68
69
70
71
72
73
75
76
77
78
79
80
81
82
83
84
85
86
87
88

1776

A rather fantastic statute ordered the doubling of the regiments into four battalions and the resulting difficulty in differentiating between them caused a splash of colour (see illustrations page 69). The other noticeable feature of this statute was the abolition of decorated pockets which were replaced by very ordinary crosswise ones.

1779 to 1786

Uniform was 'à la française' with cuffs open at at the top and seven buttons on each lapel. The regimental colours were reduced to ten, but the Royal and the Princes' regiments kept their own colours.

The regulation of October 1786 confirmed the preceding one, but gave more precise details. The details given were even more important as the uniform remained virtually unchanged for a greater part of the army until the end of the 'Empire'.

FRANCE, 1720–1736 II
CIRCA 1720 (continued)

89. Aunis—90. Beauce—91. Dauphiné—92. Vivarias—93. Luxembourg—94. Bassigny—95. Beaujolais—96. Ponthieu —97. La Marck—98. La Vallière—99. Montmorency—100. Diesbach—101. Courten—102. Appelgrehn—103. Bulkeley —104. Clare—105. Dillon—106. Rosnyvinien—107. La Ferté-Imbault—108. Blaisois—109. Gâtinais—110. Conti—111. Auxerrois—112. Agénois—113. Santerre—114. Des Landes—115. Rooth—116. Berwick—117. Enghien—118. Royal Bavière—119. Travers.

1. Soldier of the du Perche Regiment (30)—2. Grenadier of the Royal Vessels Regiment (26)—3. Lieutenant of the Piedmont Regiment (4)—4. Soldier of the King's regiment (12). The bayonet can be seen just above the sword hilt.

The unending quarrels about precedence between regiments, the formation and suppression of certain corps and the changes of name with every arrival of a new Colonel-in-Chief, makes it very difficult to trace the full details of some regiments. To describe their history, year by year, is impossible within the context of this book, but the reader will find, in addition to the notes relating to each new statute reproduced in the drawings, a few of the changes of name, rank and uniform which took place.

1791

The regiments of French infantry no longer bore the name of the King, the Queen, the princes or of any province but were given a number. The helmet was made of varnished leather or felt. The regimental colours were reduced to seven.

MODIFICATIONS FROM 1720 ONWARDS

Champagne (3) takes the place of Navarre (2) which is given the number 3; Number 21 becomes Saillans; 22, Meuse; 23, La Chesnelaye; 32, Louvignies; 48, Villars-Chandieu; 51, Hessy; 53, Saint Simon; 55, Gensac; 56, Bacqueville; 60, D'Affry; 61, Hemmel; 62, Laval. From number 65 onwards, La Marck (97) takes the place of Toulouse (65) which becomes 66 and all the regiments which follow it as far as Forez (77) go back one place. Forez becomes number 78. Cambrésis (79) keeps its number to the detriment of the Tournaisis regiment (78) which jumps to 80 and moves back by one place all the regiments which follow it as far as Ponthieu (96) which takes over the number 97 left vacant by La Marck, now number 65. Number 102, Appelgrehn, becomes Lee; Number 103, Bulkeley, becomes Clare; Number 107, La Ferté-Imbault, becomes Chartres, and lastly number 115, Rooth, is replaced by Berwick (116) and number 116 becomes d'Orington.

The hat still has braid in the same colour as the buttons. Instead of the uniformly black cockade, the King's (12) and the Alsace (36) regiments have a white and red cockade and the Saxe (45) regiment a red and blue one and the Lenck (105) regiment, a yellow one.

A certain number of regiments do seem to have had a uniform of this type with numerous variations, especially in the cut and position of the pockets, from the uniforms we have illustrated here. Except for the King's regiments the braiding and other woollen embellishments decorating the buttonholes completely disappear. Without any restrictions by the Crown, control of the uniform was only casual until the statute of 10 March 1729; this insisted that the cost of clothing had to be reduced and the general use of the same cloth was recommended.

90
91
92
93
94
95
96
97
98
99
100
101
102
103
105
106
107
108
109
110
111
112
113
114
115
116
117
118
1
2
3
4
L. & F. FUNCKEN

Some Special Corps

The French Militia

In 1726 there were some regiments and battalions of militia independent of the infantry regiments. They were composed of young men drawn from all the towns and villages of the French Provinces. This Militia was used to guard strongholds and to escort military convoys.

There were ninety-three battalions in 1726 and 123 in 1733, later organized into forty regiments and forty-three battalions. Though reduced to a hundred battalions in 1736, the militia remained stable at 112 in 1741, 110 in 1744 and once more 112 in 1748.

Royal and Provincial Grenadiers

A statute of 1744 instituted the grenadiers of the militia, with one company for each battalion. A year later these 110 companies were brought together into eleven regiments called the Royal Grenadiers. These were increased to twelve regiments in 1773 and then to thirteen in 1778.

Provincial Regiments

The French Militia formed the forty-seven 'provincial regiments in 1771, each bearing the name of a town. In 1772 the regiment of Buttafuoco[2] became the provincial regiment of Corsica, with the unusual hooded uniform shown in the illustrations on page 69.

Disbanded in 1775, the provincial regiments were re-established in 1778 with thirteen provincial artillery regiments and five staff regiments attached to the engineers.

[1] 54 according to Noirmont and Marbot.
[2] This is a family name, not the name of a locality.

FRANCE, INFANTRY 1734 TO 1757 I

The uniforms were nearly all made from off-white cloth. The hats, with the exception of two regiments, were edged with silver or gold braid, depending on the colour of the buttons. In these illustrations, the pockets have been outlined in black to make the design show up clearly, but it is not intended to represent black piping.

1. Picardy—2. Champagne—3. Navarre—4. Piedmont—5. Normandy—5a. *Idem*, officers—6. The Navy—6a. *Idem*, officers and sergeants in 1738—7. Bourbonnais—8. Rohan—9. Auvergne—10. Monaco—11. Marsan—12. King's. The coat had nine buttonholes arranged in groups of three and decorated with bright yellow braid—13. Royal—13a. *Idem* in 1740—14. Poitou—15. Lyonnais—16. Dauphin—17. Gondrin—18. Touraine—19. Anjou—20. Eu—21. Noailles—21a. *Idem* in 1740—22. Montmorin—23. Souvré—23a. *Idem in* 1740—24. Queen's—25. Limousin—26. Royal Vessels—27. Orléans—27a. *Idem* in 1740—28. La Couronne. Sometimes the hat had gold instead of silver braid—29. Brittany—29a. *Idem* in 1740—30. Du Perche—30a. *Idem* in 1740—31. Artois—32. Rochechouart—33. D'Ouroy—33a. *Idem* in 1740—34. La Sarre—35. La Fère—35a. *Idem* in 1740—36. Alsace—37. Royal Roussillon—38. Condé—39. Bourbon—40. Beauvaisis—40a. *Idem* in 1740—41. Rouergue—42. Burgundy—43. Royal Navy—44. Vermandois—45. Saxe—The 46th is not shown here as it belonged to the Royal Artillery—47. Royal Italian—47a. *Idem* in 1750—48. Bettens—48a. *Idem*, sergeants—49. Brendlé, which became Seedorff in 1749—50. Monin—50a. *Idem* in 1740—51. Tschoudy, which became Vigier in 1740—52. Languedoc—53. Puyguyon—54. Wittemer—54a. *Idem* in 1740—55. Médoc—56. Duras—57. Chaillou—58. Royal Comtois—59. Monconseil.

A. *Anspessade* of the Royal Corsican Regiment (121) in marching uniform. An *Anspessade* was a nobleman serving in the infantry. There were 12 *anspessades* in a company of 300 men—B. Soldier of the Du Perche Regiment (30) wearing marching uniform in 1740.

A
B
F. Funcken
1
2
3
4
5
5a
6
6a
7
8
9
10
11
12
13
13a
14
15
16
17
18
19
20
21
21a
22
23
23a
24
25
26
27
27a
28
29
29a
30
30a
31
32
33
33a
34
35
35a
36
37
38
39
40
40a
41
42
43
44
45
47
47a
48
48a
49
50
50a
51
52
53
54
54a
55
56
57
58
59

The Coastguard Militia

These were recruited from the inhabitants of coastal regions. From 1759 to 1778 this militia was composed of Watch companies with no uniform, unattached companies and companies of gunners. In Poitou, Aunis, Saintonge and Guyenne it even had companies of dragoons. From 1778 onwards this militia was attached to the service of seaboard batteries and took the name of *canonniers garde-côtes* (coastguard gunners).

Regiments of Recruits

Created by the statute of 1 February 1763, these thirty-one regiments of recruits were increased to thirty-three in 1765 but their numbers decreased rapidly afterwards: to seven in 1776, six in 1767 and to one only in 1768. This one survivor, formed for the colonies, itself disappeared in 1773.

FRANCE, INFANTRY 1734 TO 1757 II

60. Provence—61. Mortemart—62. La Cour-au-Chantre—63. Biron—64. Nice—65. La Marck—66. Toulouse—67. Guyenne—68. Lorraine—69. Flanders—69a. *Idem* in 1740—70. Berry—71. Béarn—72. Hainaut—73. Boulonnais—74. Angoumois—75. Périgord—76. Saintonge—77. Bigorre—78. Forez—79. Cambrésis—80. Tournaisis—81. Foix—82. Bresse—83. La Marche—84. Quercy—85. Nivernais—86. Brie—87. Soissonnais—88. Ile-de-France—89. Vexin—90. Aunis—91. Beauce—91a. *Idem* in 1740—92. Dauphiné—92a. *Idem* in 1745-93. Vivarais—93a. *Idem* in 1740—94. Luxembourg—95. Bassigny—96. Beaujolais—96a. *Idem* in 1740—97. Ponthieu—98. La Vallière—99. Montmorency—100. Diesbach—101. Courten—102. Bulkeley—103. Clare—104. Dillon—105. Appelgrehn—106. Rosnyvinien—107. Chartres—108. Blaisois—108a. *Idem* in 1740—109. Gâtinais—110. Conti—111. Auxerrois—112. Agénois—113. Santerre—114. Des Landes—115. Rooth—116. Berwick—117. Enghein—117a. *Idem* in 1740—118. Royal Bavière—118a. *Idem* in 1740—119. Karrer—120. Travers—121. Royal Corsican—122. Lowendhal—123. Royal Scottish—124. Royal Lorraine—124a. *Idem* in 1745—124b. *Idem* in 1748—124c. *Idem* in 1757—125. Bergh—126. Lally—127. Royal-Wallon. A little time after this, the regimental uniform changed to a blue coat, jacket, breeches and collar, red cuffs and linings, yellow buttons and yellow buttonholes on the coat and jacket.—128. Boufflers-Wallon, 1749. They later had red breeches and jacket with green collar and cuffs on the coat and yellow buttons (later a mixture of yellow and white as in fig. 69) and a hat edged with gold or silver—129. Royal Barrois—130. Fersen—131. Nassau-Sarrebruck—132. Royal-Cantabres—133. Ogilvy—134. Saint-Germain—135. La Dauphine—136. Royal Polish—137. Albany.

60 61 62 63 64 65 66 67 68 69 69a 70 71
72 73 74 75 76 77 78 79 80 81 82 83 84
85 86 87 88 89 90 91 91a 92 92a 93 93a 94
95 96 96a 97 98 99 100 101 102 103 104 105 106
107 108 108a 109 110 111 112 113 114 115 116 117 117a
118 118a 119 119a 120 120a 121 122 123 124 124a 124b 124c
125 126 127 128 129 130 131 132 133 134 135 136 137

Arms and Equipment

The Musket[1]

Prior to the first regulation of 1717 army muskets had only to conform to two requirements: a fixed length of barrel and the calibre.

In the early years of the century the muskets were of 18mm calibre then about 1710 it was reduced to 16mm. In 1717 the first standard model appeared when the prototypes were presented to the Council of War by the arms factories of Charleville, Maubeuge and Saint-Etienne. This was a musket with a barrel 1.593m long and a calibre of 17.5mm.

In 1728 a new model was adopted and this was to be the forerunner of all the muskets of the next 138 years. It had muzzle bands instead of the pins which, up to then, had secured the barrel to the stock.

This weapon was strongly supported by an artillery general called Jean-Florent de Vallière. He was born in Paris in 1667 and ended his career in 1759 as a Lieutenant General after he had reorganized the artillery and founded the schools which were to guarantee the superiority of the French artillery in the eighteenth century.

365,000 of this 1728 model musket with its characteristic butt *en pied de vache* (in the shape of a cow's foot) were produced. It measured 1.593mm, weighed 4.100kg and fired a 17.5mm bullet.

The 1746 and 1754 models, of which more than 200,000 were produced, had only slight modifications in comparison with the 1728 model.

The model introduced by the Duc de Choiseul in 1763, was known as the de Stainville as the Duke's previous title was the Comte de Stainville.

The de Stainville musket, which weighed 4.28kg was too heavy and a new weapon, the 1766 or 1763 'light' model was planned. This version weighed 850g less than the 1763 – a saving achieved by lightening the barrel, lock and all fittings. Both

[1] See the illustrations on page 118, numbers 73, 74 and 75.

FRANCE, 1757 I

1. Picardy—2. Champagne—3. Navarre—4. Piedmont—5. Normandy—6. The Navy—7. Latour du Pin, renamed Béarn in 1763—8. Bourbonnais (certain sources reverse the order of this and the preceding regiment)—9. Auvergne—10. Belzunce, renamed Flanders in 1763—11. Mailly, renamed Guyenne in 1763—12. King's—13. Royal—14. Poitou—15. Lyonnais—16. Dauphin—17. Vaubécourt, renamed Aunis in 1763—18. Touraine—19. Aquitaine—20. Eu—21. Saint-Chamond—22. Montmorin, renamed Ile-de-France in 1763—23. Briqueville, renamed Soissonais in 1763—24. Queen's—25. Limousin—26. Royal Vessels—27. Orléans—28. La Couronne—29. Brittany—30. Du Perche—31. Artois—32. Montbazon, renamed Berry in 1763—33. La Roche-Aymon, renamed Hainaut in 1763—34. La Sarre—35. La Fère—36. 37th or Royal Roussillon Regiment. From here on, the number of the illustration has no correlation with that of the regiment—37. 38th or Condé regiment—38. 39th or Bourbon regiment—39. 40th or Grenadiers of France (48 companies)—40. 41st or Beauvaisis regiment—41. 42nd or Rouergue regiment—42. 43rd or Burgundy—43. 44th or Marine regiment—44. 45th or Vermandois—45. 53rd or Languedoc regiment—46. 47th or regiment of fusiliers to guard the artillery—47. *Idem* from 1758 onwards—48. 54th or Talaru regiment—49. 56th or Médoc regiment—50. 57th or Cossé-Brissac regiment renamed Vivarais in 1763—51. 58th or Vastan regiment renamed Vexin in 1763—52. 59th or Royal Comtois regiment—53. 60th or Traisnel regiment renamed Beaujolais in 1763—54. 61st or Provence regiment—55. 64th or Penthièvre regiment—56. 65th or Boulonnais regiment—57. 66th or Angoumois regiment—58. 67th or Périgord regiment—59. 68th or Saintonge regiment—60. 69th or Forez regiment—61. 70th or Cambrésis regiment—62. 71st or Tournaisis regiment—63. 72nd or Foix regiment—64. 73rd or Quercy regiment—65. 74th or Nivernais regiment—66. 81st or Chartres regiment—67. 82nd or Conti regiment—68. 85th or Enghien regiment.

Regiments abolished before 1763 or incorporated in the old corps in 1749 and 1763 are: 69. 62nd or Cambis regiment—70. 64th or Rochefort regiment—71. 65th or Nice regiment—72. 68th or Guyenne regiment—73. 69th or Lorraine regiment—74. 70th or Flanders regiment—75. 71st or Berry regiment—76. 72nd or Béarn regiment—77. 73rd Hainaut regiment—78. 78th or Bigorre regiment—79. 83rd or Bresse regiment—80. 84th or La Marche regiment—81. 87th or Brie regiment—82. 88th or Soissonnais regiment—83. 89th or Ile-de-France regiment—84. Vexin (former 89th) incorporated into the 45th in 1749.

1 2 3 4 5 6 7 8 9 10 11 12 13 14
16 17 18 19 20 21 22 23 24 25 26 27 28
30 31 32 33 34 35 36 37 38 39 40 41 42
44 45 46 47 48 49 50 51 52 53 54 55 56
58 59 60 61 62 63 64 65 66 67 68 69 70
72 73 74 75 76 77 78 79 80 81 82 83 84

the 'heavy' and the 'light' models measured 1.53m and had a 17.5mm calibre. 90,000 of the first type and 200,000 of the second were produced.

In 1770 the famous 'artillery expert' Jean-Baptiste Vaquette de Gribeauval, considered the 1766 model to be too fragile and increased its weight by 600g by strengthening its lock, so producing the Gribeauval model 1770.

In 1773 the son of the great de Vallière rejected the Gribeauval model in favour of his own.

Later, this was replaced by a 1774 model, chosen by the general inspectors of the infantry on the advice of Choiseul's successor, the inept Duc d'Aiguillon. He was to be disgraced the same year on the accession of Louis XVI.

Scarcely more than 70,000 of this 1774 model were produced before it was supplanted by the 1777 model. This was manufactured under the supervision of de Gribeauval who, by insisting on a very high standard of workmanship improved the French arms industry considerably.

On the eve of the Revolution many of the old type muskets were still being used but the oldest model did not date back earlier than 1763. These muskets have become extremely rare. Many disappeared during the incessant wars of the Revolution and the Empire, and the rest were nearly all converted to the new percussion system which substituted the explosive cap for the flint. Those interested in these weapons should, if in the South of France, be sure to visit the museum of Château de l'Empéri at Salon-de-Provence. The museum, owned by Raoul and Jean Brunon has a very fine collection.

FRANCE, 1757 II

Regiments incorporated into others in 1749: 1. Aunis (ex 90th) incorporated into the 53rd or Languedoc Regt—2. Beauce (ex 91st) incorporated into the 54th or Talaru Regt—3. Dauphiné (ex 92nd) incorporated into the 56th or Médoc Regt—4. Vivarais (ex 93rd) incorporated into the 57th or Cossé-Brissac Regt—5. Luxembourg (ex 94th) incorporated into the 58th or Vastan Regt—6. Bassigny (ex 95th) incorporated into the 59th or Royal Comtois Regt—7. Beaujolais (ex 96th) incorporated into the 60th or Durfort Regt—8. Ponthieu (ex 97th) incorporated into the 61st or Provence Regt—9. D'Escars or Des Cars (ex 97th) incorporated into the 62nd or Tournaisis Regt—10. Montmorency (ex 99th) incorporated into the 64th or Contaut-Biron Regt—11. Rosnyvinien (ex 106th) incorporated into the 65th or Nice Regt—12. Blaisois (ex 108th) incorporated into the 68th or Guyenne Regt—13. Gâtinais (ex 109th) incorporated into the 69th or Lorraine Regt—14. Auxerrois (ex 111th) incorporated into the 70th or Flanders Regt—15. Agénois (ex 112th) incorporated into the 71st or Berry Regt—16. Santerre (ex 113th) incorporated into the 72nd or Béarn Regt—17. Des Landes (ex 114th) incorporated into the 73rd or Hainaut Regt.

18. French Militia, formed in 1726 and consisting of 112 battalions. It was abolished in 1762—19. Grenadiers of France consisting of 11 regiments in 1744—10. Royal Lorraine (Lorraine Militia)—21. Royal Barrois (Lorraine Militia).

Swiss regiments: 22. 49th or d'Erlach Regt—23. 50th or Boccard Regt—24. 51st or Reding Regt—25. 52nd or Castellas Regt—26. 55th or Wittemer Regt—27. 63rd or Planta Regt—28. 77th or Diesbach Regt—29. 78th or Courten Regt—30. 87th or Mayenfeld Regt—31. 90th or Diesbach Regt.

German regiments: 32. 36th or Alsace Regt—33. 46th or Bentheim Regt—34. 66th or La Marck Regt—35. 80th or Royal Swedish Regt—36. 86th or Royal Bavière Regt—37. 89th or Nassau-Usingen Regt—38. 91st or Ardennes Regt (not German, created in 1758)—39. 92nd or Royal-Deux-Ponts Regt.

40. 48th or Royal Italian Regt (uniform worn until 1750)—41. *Idem* from 1750 to 1762 (one also finds the waistcoat, breeches and cocked part of the hat in blue)—42. 93rd or Eptingen Regt (Swiss regiment created in 1758).

Irish regiments: 43. 77th or Bulkeley Regt—44. 78th or Clare Regt—45. 79th or Dillon Regt—46. 83rd or Rooth Regt—47. Fitzjames Regt.

Regiments created since 1740 and abolished in 1762: 48. Lowendhal, German regiment—49. Nassau-Sarrebruck, German regiment—50. Bergh, German regiment—51. Royal Polish, German regiment—52. The Count of Saint-Germain's German regiment—53. La Dauphine, Saxon regiment—54. Royal Scots—55. Ogilvy, Scottish regiment—56. Lally-Tollendal, Irish regiment—57. Karrer, Swiss regiment—58. Royal Corsican—59. Buttafuoco, Corsican regiment—60. Royal Wallon—61. Boufflers-Wallon—62. Vierzet—63. Horion.

Flags: 64. Grenadiers of France—65. Royal Grenadiers—66. Royal Lorraine—67. Militia—68. Royal Barrois.

1
2
3
4
5
6
7
8
9
10
11
12
13
14
15
16
17
18
19
20
21
65
66
67
68
23
24
25
26
27
28
29
30
31
32
33
34
35
37
38
39
40
41
42
43
44
45
46
47
48
49
51
52
53
54
55
56
57
58
59
60
61
62
63

Munition

Originally the soldier had to carry bullets, powder and the fine priming powder in separate containers. The invention of the first cartridge containing the bullet and 8g of gunpowder reduced the number of steps needed to load the musket.

The time saved was considerable but it was still necessary to prime the lock from a powder horn. About 1744, improvements in the manufacture of the powder permitted the production of a cartridge containing powder fine enough to be used for priming. From that time on, the loading in '12 temps et 17 mouvements' gave the flint lock weapon a rate of fire of about three shots a minute.

The method used for loading and the workings of the flint lock are explained in the text and drawings of the muskets of the British Infantry (see pages 118 and 119).

It was often necessary for the soldier to clear the touch-hole with an implement called a 'pricker' and he had to change the flint after twenty shots. In wet weather the musket was particularly liable to misfire. The musket had a range of about 160 metres.

Equipment

The most important piece of the foot soldier's equipment was the *fourniment*, a term which incorporated the powder flask, the powder horn for the priming powder and the bullets. All this was hung from a buff leather shoulder strap, about 14cm wide. Later a leather pouch was developed, containing a wooden block drilled with nineteen holes. Each compartment held one paper cartridge. This container was called after its contents *cartouche* (cartridge) and although the term *giberne* appeared in a work by Puységur in 1748, the order *Ouvrez la cartouche* (open cartridge pouches) was still used, certainly until 1769.

The new cartridge pouch, the giberne, did not completely replace the old *fourniment*, so the soldier was not without ammunition even when he had used up his supply of cartridges.

At this time certain regiments carried an oblong cartridge box which held only ten cartridges. It was carried on the belt over the stomach, a style called 'being armed like a Corsican'.

The introduction of the complete cartridge meant that the other cumbersome loading materials were abandoned.

The bayonet and the sword, slung from the belt, were the close combat weapons of the foot soldier. Grenadiers carried the wide sabre instead of the sword.

The grenadier's cartridge box was larger than that of the ordinary companies and was made of soft cowhide. It was called the 'grenadière' as it originally contained grenades, but these had been used less and less since the battle of Steinkerque[1] in 1692. In the early years of the eighteenth century, the considerable increase in the power of the volley fire of the infantry made grenades obsolete.

The grenade pouch was also designed to hold a short, but strong axe which the grenadier carried in place of the various digging tools (ten to each company) carried by the fusiliers.

[1] North of Soignies, in Belgium, known today as Steenkerque. Yet another victory for the Marshal of Luxembourg (see pages 26 and 44).

FRANCE, REGIMENTAL FLAGS II

1. Mortemart—2. La Cour-au-Chantre (Swiss regiment)—3. Biron, 1717 to 1762—4. Nice, 1691 to 1752—5. Lamarck (German regiment), 1697 to 1791—6. Penthièvre, 1737 to 1791—7. Guyenne, 1684 to 1762—8. Lorraine, 1684 to 1762—9. Flanders, 1684 to 1762—10. Berry, 1684 to 1762—11. Béarn, 1684 to 1762—12. Hainaut—13. Boulonnais, 1684 to 1791—14. Angoumois, 1684 to 1791—15. Périgord, 1684 to 1775—16. Saintonge, 1684 to 1791—17. Bigorre, 1684 to 1763—18. Forez, 1684 to 1776—19. Cambrésis, 1684 to 1775—20. Tournaisis, 1684 to 1775—21. Foix, 1702 to 1709—22. Bresse, 1683 to 1763—23. La Marche, 1684 to 1763—24. Quercy, 1684 to 1776—25. Nivernais, 1684 to 1763—26. Brie, 1727 to 1762—27. Soissonnais, 1684 to 1762—28. Ile-de-France, 1762 to 1791—29. Vexin, 1684 to 1749—30. Aunis, 1684 to 1749.

2
3
4
5
7
8
9
10
12
13
14
15
17
18
19
20
22
23
24
25
27
28
29
30

The Knapsack

The first model was made of strong canvas waterproofed with linseed oil. It fastened with a little strap like a miller's bag. It was slung from braces, a long strap crossing the chest from the right shoulder and a shorter one from the left shoulder.

In 1766 it was replaced by a calfskin bag measuring 48 × 33cm, with fur on the outside. Later a forage bag was added which could also be used as a sleeping bag.

In 1775 a new model was issued, similar to the preceding one, but with the inside divided into compartments. It was fastened with three straps.

Arms of the Officers and Sergeants

The special weapon of the sergeants of the fusiliers, apart from the sword, was the halberd measuring 2.14m overall.

The grenadier sergeants carried a musket with a bayonet, like their men. In 1758, fusilier sergeants abandoned the halberd which was then mainly used for measuring the correct distances between rows, and also adopted the musket.

At the beginning of the century the officers were armed with swords and with a spontoon which measured between 2.65 and 2.97m. It was more a mark of rank than a weapon and was carried by colonels, lieutenant-colonels, and captains.

The lieutenants and subordinate officers carried a shorter spontoon, which measured 2.37m. The order of 1710 replaced them with the bayonet and musket which was shorter, lighter and of better quality than those carried by the troops. These officers are often called the *officiers porte-fusils* or musket-bearing officers.

In 1756 according to Leinhart and Humbert (1767 according to Noirmont and Marbot) the spontoons were discarded by the senior officers who retained the sword which measured 80.9cm. Subordinate officers kept the musket and the 70.3cm sword. The musket was withdrawn in 1787.

Originally sword hilts were either silver or gold but they were uniformly gold from 1786 onwards. The sword-knot was made of gold thread regardless of the metal of the epaulet, until 1767, after which time it was mixed with flame coloured silk thread. In 1786 a statute gave the precise pro-

FRANCE, 1762 AND 1767 I

1. Picardy—2. Champagne—3. Navarre—3a. Navarre in 1767—4. Piedmont—5. Normandy—5a. Normandy in 1767—6. The Navy—6a. The Navy in 1767—7. Béarn—8. Bourbonnais—9. Auvergne—10. Flanders—11. Guyenne—12. King's—13. Royal—14. Poitou—15. Lyonnais—16. Dauphin—17. Aunis—17a. Aunis in 1767—18. Touraine—19. Aquitaine—20. Eu—21. Dauphiné—22. Ile-de-France—23. Soissonnais—24. The Queen's—25. Limousin—26. Royal Vessels—27. Orléans—27a. Orléans in 1767—28. La Couronne—29. Brittany—29a. *Idem* in 1767—29b. Another version of the Brittany regiment—30. Gardes-lorraines—30a. Gardes-lorraines in 1766—31. Artois—32. Berry—33. Hainaut—33a. Hainaut in 1767—34. La Sarre—34a. La Sarre in 1767—35. La Fère—35a. La Fère in 1767—36. Alsace—36a. Alsace in 1767—37. Royal-Roussillon—38. Condé—38a. Condé in 1767—39. Bourbon—40. French Grenadiers—41. Beauvaisis—41a. Beauvaisis in 1767—42. Rouergue—43. Burgundy—44. Royal Navy—45. Vermandois—45a. Vermandois in 1767—46. Anhalt—47. Royal Italian—48. D'Erlach—49. Boccard—50. Reding—51. Castellas—52. Languedoc—52a. Languedoc in 1767—53. Beauce—53a. Beauce in 1767.

The figures repeating those which illustrate the statute of 1762 give only the changes made to the uniform by the statute of 1767. The numbers of the drawings from 1 to 45 correspond to the rank of the regiment but from 46 to 54 one must be added to each number to obtain the regiment's number.

56 to 59 Evolution of the uniform from 1720 to 1736 and from 1757 to 1767. The Royal Navy is taken as an example, see also fig. 44.

60. Tricorn hats of the middle of the eighteenth century.
61. Grenadiers hat around 1760.

2 3 3a 4 5 5a 6 6a 7 8 9 10 11
13 14 15 16 17 17a 18 19 20 21 22 23 24
56 57 58 59 60 61
26 27 27a 28 29 29a 29b 30 30a 31 32 33 33a
34a 35 35a 36 36a 37 38 38a 39 40 41 41a 42
44 45 45a 46 47 48 49 50 51 52 52a 53 53a

portions of gold and of silk to be used and this had to match the epaulet. The tassel and its fringe followed the same rule, with the fringe a miniature version of the epaulet fringe.

This rather expensive style of decoration wore out very quickly as it rubbed against the breeches, which it blackened and it also interfered with the use of the sword. Therefore, from about 1792 the sword-knot was only worn with full dress uniform.

A new model in white thread was authorized, but proved useless because it became dirty very quickly and did not show the wearer's rank. Eventually the knot was abolished altogether.

Sappers

It was Vauban, the expert on defence and siege warfare who persuaded the court to form the first company of sappers in 1668. The artillery sappers should not be confused with the ones described here.

In 1710 they were given the name of 'tool carriers'. At that time there were only six to a regiment and their usefulness had had to be proved during the war of Spanish Succession.[1]

The statute of 19 January 1747 established ten 'axe carrying soldiers' in each company of grenadiers, after the campaigns of the War of Austrian Succession,[2] which France had entered into in 1741. This campaign had shown the need for specialists who could clear the way for the infantry through the obstacles placed in their way by the enemy.

On 19 April 1766 each infantry company had two sappers called 'carpenter soldiers' posted to them. In the following year they were allowed to wear a special headdress; a fur cap like that of the grenadiers, but shorter and without the badge.

[1] A war caused by the succession of Philip v, grandson of Louis xiv to the Spanish throne. France confronted Austria, England and the United Provinces (1701 to 1714).

[2] A war in which France, Prussia and Bavaria opposed Austria who was later supported by England (1740 to 1748).

FRANCE 1762 AND 1767 II

The sketches opposite, numbered 1 to 39 represent the last regiments on the list from the 55th to the 92nd.

1. Waldner—1a. Waldner in 1767—2. Médoc—3. Vivarais—4. Vexin—5. Royal Comtois—6. Beaujolais—7. Provence—7a. Provence in 1767—8. D'Arbonnier—9. La Marck—9a. La Marck in 1767—10. Penthièvre—11. Boulonnais—12. Angoumois—13. Périgord—14. Saintonge—15. Forez—16. Cambrésis—16a. Cambrésis in 1767—17. Tournaisis—17a. Tournaisis in 1767—18. Foix—19. Quercy—20. La Marche—21. Diesbach—22. Courten. Sometimes a blue collar was worn; and for 1767 collars, lapels, cuffs and shoulder flaps were in green—23. Bulkeley—24. Betagh—25. Dillon—25a. Dillon in 1767—26. Royal Swedish—27. Chartres—28. Conti—28a. Conti in 1767—29. Rooth—30. Berwick, little worn in this form. The collar, lapels and cuffs were normally black. See also fig 41—31. Berwick in 1767—32. Engheim—32a. Enghien in 1767—33. Royal Bavière—34. Salis—35. Nassau. In 1767 the collar, lapels and facings were white—36. Lochmann—37. Bouillon—38. Royal Deux-Ponts—38a. Royal Deux-Ponts in 1767—39. Eptingen.

40. Uniform of the Alsace regiment in 1764 (according to Rigo)—41. Uniform of the Berwick regiment. Cuff flaps on the sleeves are seen for the first time (1768).

Special Uniforms: 42. Militia, 1726 to 1762 (basic colour white for the Lorraine Militia)—43. Militia drummer—44 to 46. Royal Grenadiers in 1744—47. Provincial regiments in 1772—48. Recruit regiment formed in 1763 and abolished in 1768—49. First uniform of the Corsican provincial regiment (1772)—50. Second uniform of the Corsican provincial regiment (1786)—51 to 53. Coastguard Militias—foot-soldier, gunner and dragoon—54. Provincial regiments in 1786—55. Corsican regiment in 1786.

The 1762 statute, also known as the Choiseul Statute greatly changed the uniforms. Even the old regiments the 'old timers' and the 'little old-timers' lost their traditional privileges, retaining only their rank and the off-white of their former uniform. Each regiment received a number which was shown on the buttons.

1 1a 2 3 4 5 6 7 7a 8 9 9a 10 11
13 14 15 16 16a 17 17a 18 19 20 21 22 23
25 25a 26 27 28 28a 29 30 31 32 32a 33 34
35 36 37 38 38a 39
40
41
43 44 45 46 47 48 49 50 51 52 53 54 55

They could be distinguished by their long aprons, made of black skin, which could be looped up by means of a clasp. The 'carpenter soldier' carried a sabre, the blade of which also served as a saw. He also carried an axe on his shoulder.

Up to this time the sappers had only served during war and they were disbanded by statute on 19 January 1771. They were re-established in 1778 and it was decided two years later to keep them even in peace time. Their apron was changed to white and their cap replaced by the usual style of hat. On their sleeves they wore the emblem of two crossed axes, in blue or white depending on the basic colour of the uniform.

Drummers, drum majors and musicians

The Drummers

Originally considered as servants, the drummers of the early eighteenth century had many styles of uniform. Their coat, or tunic, was nothing more than their captain's livery up until the time when Louis XIV decided that all the army should wear only his own arms. Exceptions were made in the case of regiments under the control of a Colonel-in-Chief, the Queen, Princes of the blood royal or regiments supplied from abroad. In the majority of regiments the drummers were dressed in a blue coat, with crimson and white braid on the collar, cuffs and pockets and along the seams.

In 1720 they either had coats in the colours of their Colonel-in-Chief or, more often, a blue waistcoat trimmed with the braid of the royal livery along the seams to the belt and up to the leather collar, which supported the drum.

This kind of trimming lasted without any notable changes until the Seven Years' War.[1] The arrangement of the braid varied from one regiment to another and in 1757 it was to be found as

[1] Seven Years' War (1756 to 1763). By an amazing reversal of alliances (see notes, page 68, on war of Austrian Succession) France found herself on the side of Austria and Russia against England and Prussia.

FRANCE, REGIMENTAL FLAGS III

1. Beauce, 1684 to 1749—2. Dauphiné, 1684 to 1749—3. Vivarais—4. Luxembourg, 1684 to 1749—5. Bassigny, 1684 to 1749—6. Beaujolais, 1685 to 1749—7. Ponthieu, 1685 to 1749—8. La Vallière, 1688 to 1749—9. Bauffremont, 1689 to 1749—10. Diesbach (Swiss regiment), 1721 to 1791—11. Courten, 1721 to 1791—12. Bulkeley (Irish regiment), 1690 to 1775—13. Clare (Irish regiment), 1690 to 1775—14. Dillon (Irish regiment), 1690 to 1791—15. Applegrehn (German regiment), 1734 to 1756—16. Rosnyvinien, 1733 to 1749—17. Chartres, 1691 to 1791—18. Blaisois, 1692–1749—19. Gâtinais, 1692–1702—20. Conti, 1692 to 1791—21. Auxerrois, 1692 to 1749—22. Agénois, 1692 to 1749—23. Santerre, 1692 to 1705—24. Des Landes, 1693 to 1749—25. Rooth (Irish regiment), 1720 to 1791—26. Berwick (Irish regiment), 1720 to 1791—27. Royal Bavière (German regiment), 1709 to 1780—28. Karrer (Swiss regiment), 1735 to 1763—29. Royal Corsican, 1776 to 1780—30. Gardes-lorraines, 1766 to 1791.

2
3
4
5
7
8
9
10
Fidelitati & Honore
Fidelitati & Honore
12
13
14
IN HOC SIGNO VINCES
IN HOC SIGNO VINCES
IN HOC SIGNO VINCES
15
17
18
19
20
22
23
24
25
IN HOC SIGNO VINCES
27
28
Fidelitati & Honore
Terra & mari
29
30

piping around the buttonholes and along the seams of the sleeves. In 1775 it was used in circles and stripes on the sleeves, and lapels were in the regimental colour. As the illustrations show, there were many variations.

The law of 4 September 1792 brought an end to the wearing of the King's livery.

As each company had a drummer and as a regiment might have from one to four battalions of seventeen companies, some regiments had as many as sixty-eight drummers.

The barrels of the early drums were made of wood – either oak or chestnut. Skins were stretched onto the barrels with the help of braces made of two circles of wood which were pierced. Threaded through the holes were cords, bound with buff leather. The muffled tone of this type of drum was improved by a cord stretched across the skin. At that time the drum measured approximately 82cm high and 82cm wide which meant that the drummer had to carry it very high on the left side in order to be able to play it while marching. A smaller version must have been adopted towards the middle of the century because the statute of 25 April 1767 fixed the height of the barrel at 33cm and its width at approximately 37cm. According to other sources, the drum at the time was 55cm high and 55cm wide. There was one important innovation, the barrel was, by now, made of copper and weighed about 3.500kg.

In 1775 the drummer could only wear the number of his regiment, as the coats of arms of the King or the colonel were forbidden. The statute of the 1 October 1786 completely banned any kind of decoration on the barrel of the drum.

Drum Majors

At the beginning of the century the drum major wore a uniform which differed only from that of the ordinary drummer by having silver on the cuffs. He carried a stick, originally an instrument of punishment, but then used as a means of tapping out the rhythm and as a badge of office.

Their uniform did change a great deal. Cuffs, decorated with a double band of livery braid in 1767 were changed to gold braid in 1775. The regulation of 1779 reduced this to a single band and expressly forbade any other decoration.

FRANCE, STATUTE OF 1775

As in the other illustrations the numbers indicate the rank of each regiment.
1. Picardy—2. Champagne—3. Navarre—4. Piedmont—5. Normandy—6. The Navy—7. Bourbonnais—8. Béarn—9. Auvergne—10. Flanders—11. Guyenne—12. The King's—13. Royal—14. Brie—15. Poitou—16. Bresse—17. Lyonnais—18. Du Maine—19. Dauphin—20. Du Perche—21. Aunis—22. Bassigny—23. Touraine—24. Savoie-Carignan—25. Aquitaine—26. Anjou—27. Nivernais—28. Dauphiné—29. Ile-de-France—30. Soissonnais—31. The Queen's—32. Limousin—33. Royal Vessels—34. Orléans—35. La Couronne—36. Brittany—37. Lorraine—38. Artois—39. Berry—40. Hainaut—41. La Sarre—42. La Fère—43. Alsace—44. Royal Roussillon—45. Condé—46. Bourbon—47. Beauvaisis—48. Rouergue—49. Burgundy—50. Royal Navy—51. Vermandois—52. Anhalt—53, which became the Royal Artillery, is missing—54. Royal Italian—55. D'Erlach—56. Boccard—57. Sonnenberg—58. Castellas—59. Languedoc—60. Beauce—61. Waldner—62. Médoc—63. Vivarais—64. Vexin—65. Royal Comtois—66. Beaujolais—67. Monsieur's (here wearing the epaulets of the grenadiers)—68. D'Aulbonne—69. La Marck—70. Penthièvre—71. Boulonnais—72. Angoumois—73. La Marche—74. Saintonge—75. Foix—76. Quercy—77. Diesbach—78. Courten—79. Dillon—80. Berwick—81. Royal-Swedish—82. Chartres—83. Conti—84. Enghien—85. No regiment of that number—86. Royal-Bavière—87. Salis—88. Royal Corsican—89. Nassau—90. Lochmann—91. Bouillon—92. Royal Deux-Ponts—93. Eptingen.

A. Corporal of a foreign regiment in 1745. The braid was white on blue or red uniforms—B. Lieutenant of the Bourbon Grenadier Regiment in 1772—C. Corporal with the stripes showing 8 years' re-enlisted service; also worn by ordinary soldiers—D. Lieutenant of the La Marck Regiment in 1775.

A
B
C
D
1 2 3 4 5 6 7 8 9 10
11 12 13 14 15 16 17 18 19 20
21 22 23 24 25 26 27 28 29 30
31 32 33 34 35 36 37 38 39 40
41 42 43 44 45 46 47 48 49 50
51 52 54 55 56 57 58 59 60 61
62 63 64 65 66 67 68 69 70 71
72 73 74 75 76 77 78 79 80 81
82 83 84 86 87 88 89 90 91 92 93

Finally in 1786 the livery braid was permitted on the waist seams as was a double band of silver braid on the cuffs. Other trimmings and the fringed epaulets which many drum majors had adopted were forbidden.

Musicians

Until 1777 or thereabouts, the only military musicians were the pipers and the clarinet players. The clarinet then in use was so rudimentary that it was liable to change tone with each octave. In 1777, horns and other brass instruments were added. This innovation marked the starting point for modern military music.

The musician's uniform was similar to that of the drummer until 1766 when it was slightly modified by the abandonment of livery braid and the adoption of silver braid on the cuffs. This braid matched the colour of the buttons in 1779 but was once again silver and 22.5mm wide in 1786. From 1767, the master of music could be distinguished by the extra braid on the collar.

FRANCE, REGULATION OF 1776

Rigo, the expert on uniforms, wrote that the doubling of the regiments to four battalions showed an astonishing lack of taste. As only a certain number of classical 'regimental colours' was at their disposal, iron grey and flax grey were introduced. This was insufficient and the uniforms were mixed up with no regard to the most long-established traditions. This heresy was not tolerated for long and in 1779 a new statute appeared which brought clear, precise logic to the situation.

1. Picardy—2. Provence—3. Champagne—4. Austrasie—5. Navarre—6. Armagnac—7. Piedmont—8. Blaisois—9. Normandy—10. Neustrie—11. The Navy—12. Auxerrois—13. Béarn—14. Agénois—15. Bourbonnais—16. Forez—17. Auvergne—18. Gâtinais—19. Flanders—20. Cambrésis—21. Guyenne—22. Viennese—23. The King's—24. Royal—25. Brie—26. Poitou—27. Bresse—28. Lyonnais—29. Du Maine—30. Dauphin—31. DuPerche—32. Aunis—32a. *Idem* variation—33. Bassigny—33a. *Idem*, variation—34. Touraine—35. Savoie-Carignan—36. Aquitaine—37. Anjou—38. Nivernais—39. Dauphiné—40. Ile-de-France—41. Soissonnais—42. The Queen's—43. Limousin—44. Royal vessels—45. Orléans—46. La Couronne—47. Brittany—48. Lorraine—49. Artois—50. Berry—51. Hainaut—52. La Sarre—52a. *Idem*, variation—53. La Fère—54. Alsace—55. Royal Roussillon—56. Condé—57. Bourbon—58. Beauvaisis—59. Rouergue—60. Burgundy—61. Royal Navy—62. Vermandois—63. Anhalt—64. Royal Italian—65. D'Erlach—66. Boccard—66a. *Idem*, variation—67 is missing—68. Sonnenberg—69. Castellas—70. Languedoc—71. Beauce—71a. *Idem*, variation—72. Waldner—73. Médoc—74. Vivarais—75. Vexin—76. Royal-Comtois—77. Beaujolais—78. Monsieur's—(title given to eldest of the King's brothers)—78a. *Idem*, variation—79. D'Aulbonne—80. La Marck—81. Penthièvre—82. Boulonnais—82a. *Idem*, variation—83. Angoumois—84. Conti—85. Saintonge—86. Foix—87. Rohan-Soubise—88. Diesbach—89. Courten—90. Dillon—91. Berwick—92. Royal Swedish—93. Chartres—94. Barrois—95. Walsh—96. Enghien—97. Royal Bavière—The 98th is missing—99. Salis—100. Royal Corsican. The Royal Corsicans had yellow braided shoulder straps as well as a yellow facing decorated with blue fleurs-de-lis.—101. Naussau—101a. *Idem*, variation—102. Lochmann—103. Bouillon—104. Royal Deux-Ponts—105. Eptingen—

A. Officer of the Bourbon Regiment in 1775—B. Officer of the King's Regiment in 1776—C. Soldier of the Royal la Couronne Regiment in 1776. The buff-leather strap across the chest was first worn at this time.

A
B
C
D
& F. FUNCKEN
1 2 3 4 5 6 7 8 9 10
11 12 13 14 15 16 17 18 19 20
21 22 23 24 25 26 27 28 29 30
31 32 32 a 33 33 a 34 35 36 37 38
39 40 41 42 43 44 45 46 47 48
49 50 51 52 52 a 53 54 55 56 57
58 59 60 61 62 63 64 65 66 66 a
68 69 70 71 71 a 72 73 74 75 76 77
78 78 a 79 80 81 82 82 a 83 84 85 86 87 88 89 90
91 92 93 94 95 96 97 99 100 101 101 a 102 103 104 105

Sergeants and Corporals

As the difference in uniform made the N.C.O.s conspicuous, they were prime targets on the battlefield and suffered heavy casualties. As a result they began to wear badges of rank which were not quite so obvious.

1720

In 1720 the sergeants wore three decorations in gold or fine silver braid on cuff buttonholes, or a single band of silver on the cuff itself. Corporals had the same emblems but in white, yellow, red or blue woollen braid.

1747

In 1747 the woollen band on the cuff was reserved for the *anspessades*[1] and sergeants and corporals were distinguished by the three gold, silver or woollen decorations corresponding to the cuff buttons. It is not known what distinction was made on the sleeves of regiments which had more than three buttons on the cuff.

1762

Sergeants had their cuffs decorated with gold or silver braid about 28mm wide. Quartermasters were distinguished by a double gold band, sewn onto the arm. Corporals had a double band of goatskin on each cuff.

1767

The regulation of 25 April 1767 gave sergeants a distinctive badge – a blue wool trimming on the cuffs of white uniforms and a double braid of white thread on red or blue uniforms. Alex Cart, in his interesting book *Uniforms of the French regiments from Louis XV to the present day*, describes it as a single braid running from one seam to the other on the sleeve.

Quartermasters: same arrangement, as well as two similar bands above the elbow.

Corporals: two bands of blue woollen braid.

[1] See the note on page 36.

FRANCE, INFANTRY 1779 I

With the exception of the Picardy, Royal and Princes' regiments, the French regiments are classed in sixes in their order of seniority. Each of the ten classes represents two divisions of three regiments.

O. Picardy.

A. First series: 1. 2nd or Provence Regt—2. 3rd or Piedmont Regt—3. 4th or Blaisois Regt—4. 5th or Navarre Regt—5. 6th or Armagnac Regt—6. 7th or Champagne Regt.
B. Second series: 1. 8th or Austrasie Regt—2. 9th or Normandy Regt—3. 10th or Neustrie Regt—4. 11th regiment, The Navy—5. 12th or Auxerrois Regt—6. 13th or Bourbonnais Regt.
C. Third series: 1. 14th or Forez Regt—2. 15th or Béarn Regt—3. 16th or Agénois Regt—4. 17th or Auvergne Regt—5. 18th or Gâtinais Regt—6. 19th or Flanders Regt.
D. Fourth series: 1. 20th or Cambrésis Regt—2. 21st or Guyenne Regt—3. 22nd or Viennese Regt—4. 25th or Brie Regt—5. 26th or Poitou Regt—6. 27th or Bresse Regt.
E. Fifth series: 1. 28th or Lyonnais Regt—2. 29th or Du Maine Regt—3. 31st or Du Perche Regt—4. 32nd or Aunis Regt—5. 33rd or Bassigny Regt—6. 34th or Touraine Regt.
F. Sixth series: 1. 35th or Savoie-Carignan Regt—2. 36th or Aquitaine Regt—3. 37th or Anjou Regt—4. 38th or Maréchal de Turenne Regt—5. 39th or Dauphiné Regt—6. 40th or Ile-de-France Regt.
G. Seventh series: 1. 41st or Soissonnais Regt—2. 43rd or Limousin Regt—3. 47th or Brittany Regt—4. 48th or Lorraine Regt—5. 50th or Berry Regt—6. 51st or Hainaut Regt.
H. Eighth series: 1. 52nd or La Sarre Regt—2. 53rd or La Fère Regt—3. 58th or Beauvaisis Regt—4. 59th or Rouergue Regt—5. 60th or Burgundy Regt—6. 62nd or Vermandois Regt.
I. Ninth series: 1. 70th or Languedoc Regt—2. 71st or Beauce Regt—3. 73rd or Médoc Regt—4. 74th or Vivarais Regt—5. 75th or Vexin Regt—6. 77th or Beaujolais Regt.
J. Tenth series: 1. 82nd or Boulonnais Regt—2. 83rd or Angoumois Regt—3. 85th or Saintonge Regt—4. 86th or Foix Regt—5. 87th or Rohan-Soubise Regt—6. 94th or Barrois Regt.

Shoulder straps, although often shown in the style given in the preceding diagrams, were buttoned near to the sleeve seam as shown in the following figures: 7. Fusilier. The shoulder straps were trimmed with the colour of their class or series—8. Grenadier—9. Chasseur.

10. Fusilier's hat. The cockade is hidden by the front point—11. Grenadier's hat with its red 'carrot'—12. Chasseur's hat seen from behind with its distinctive green pompom.

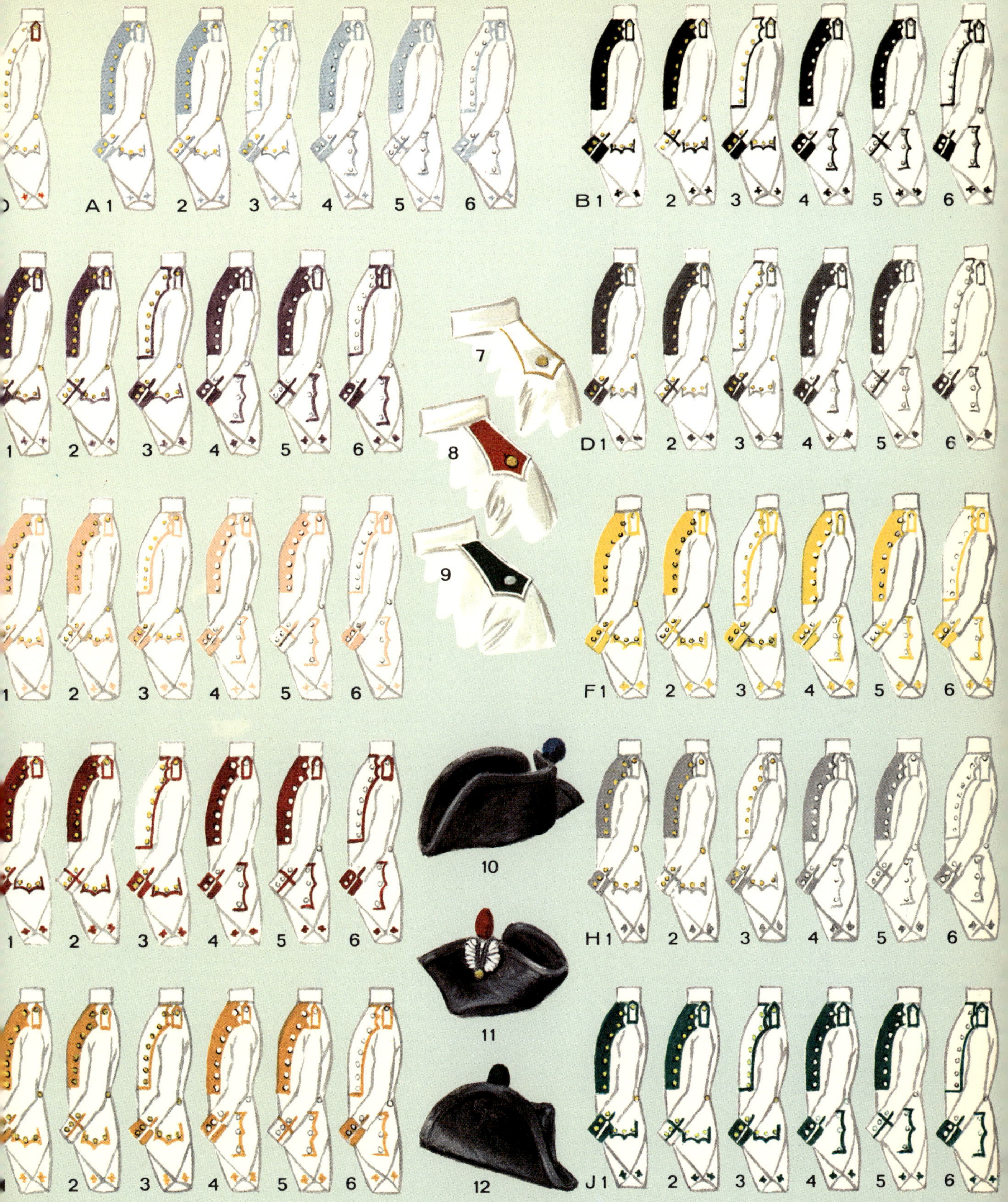

A 1 2 3 4 5 6
B 1 2 3 4 5 6
1 2 3 4 5 6
7
8
D 1 2 3 4 5 6
1 2 3 4 5 6
9
F 1 2 3 4 5 6
1 2 3 4 5 6
10
H 1 2 3 4 5 6
11
2 3 4 5 6
12
J 1 2 3 4 5 6

1779

Sergeant-majors: a double band of silver braid, 22.5mm wide. The first on the cuffs, the second on the forearm about 1.5cm above the first.

Quartermaster Clerks: two silver braids arranged as above but on the forearm only.

Sergeants: a single gold or silver band 1.5cm above the cuffs; on white uniforms these were piped with the distinctive colour of the regiment.

Gentlemen Cadets: this position had been created three hundred years before to accommodate the younger sons of noblemen who, because of the system whereby the eldest son inherited, were deprived of any property from their fathers. There was one gentleman cadet per company. Their rank was shown by a silver braid 13.5mm wide around the collar. In 1779 they had epaulets in gold or silver braid according to the colour of the buttons.

Corporals: they had a double band of blue woollen braid, above and parallel to the cuffs; the first 13.5mm and the second 7mm from the cuff on white uniforms. These markings were white on blue or red uniforms.

FRANCE, INFANTRY IN 1779 II

A. Royal Regiments. They had royal blue as their regimental colour and the eight regiments were divided into two groups or divisions of four.
First group: 1. 23rd or King's Regt—2. 24th or Royal Regt—3. 30th or Dauphin Regt—4. 44th or Royal Vessels Regt—Second group: 5. 46th or La Couronne Regt—6. 46th or Royal Roussillon Regt—7. 61st Regiment, the Royal Navy—8. Royal Comtois Regt.

B. The Princes' Regiments. These ten regiments had scarlet as their regimental colour and were divided into two groups of five. First group: 1. 42nd or Queen's Regt—2. 45th or Orléans Regt—3. 49th or Artois Regt. In 1785 it became the 35th or Duc d' Angoulême Regt—4. 56th or Condé Regt—5. 57th or Bourbon Regt—Second group: 6. 78th or Monsieur's Regt—7. 81st or Penthièvre Regt—8. 84th or Conti Regt—9. 91st or Chartres Regt—10. 96th or Enghien Regt.

C. Foreign Regiments had kept the same uniform as in 1776 except for: 1. Nassau—2. Royal Deux-Ponts—3. Royal Corsican.

REGULATION OF 1786

D. 1. 1st or Colonel General Regt. The Prince of Condé, having been appointed Colonel General of the Infantry in 1780, the Picardy regiment took the name of Colonel General. The 2nd regiment of Infantry, the former Provence regiment, was rechristened Picardy—2. Picardy—3. 4th or Provence Regt—4. 35th or Duc d'Angoulême Regt—5. 46th or La Couronne Regt—6. 49th or Artois Regt—Note that the Duc d'Angoulême's regiment, given the number 35, did not occupy first place in the princes' regiments represented here in series B. It therefore took the place of the Artois (49th) regiment without changing the classification, after the Queen's (42nd) and the Orléans (45th) regiments. The Comte d'Artois regiment adopted the uniform of the Savoie-Carignan (35th) regiment (see preceding page, series F, fig 1) and so the Artois regiment, although 49th, became the first of the regiments having daffodil yellow as its regimental colour. Gâtinais (preceding page, series C, fig 5) took the name of Royal Auvergne.

E. Modifications made to foreign regiments by the 1776 regulation:
1. 66th or Ernest Regt—2. 68th or Sonnenberg Regt—3. 69th or Castellas Regt—4. 72nd or Vigier Regt—5. 79th or Châteauvieux Regt—6. 88th or Diesbach Regt—7.89th or Courten Regt—8. 98th or Salis-Grisons—9. 99th or Steiner Regt—10. 90th or Dillon Regt—11. 97th or Royal Hessen-Darmstadt Regt—12. 106th or Montreal Regt. Formed on 10 December 1778, it became the property of the Count of Montreal in 1784—13. 107th or Royal Liégeois, formed on 18 November 1787 and belonging to the Prince Bishop of Liège—14. 106th or Montreal Regt between 1784 and 1785.

Decorations of the facings: 15. Fusiliers—16. Grenadiers—17. Chasseurs. In most cases they were in regimental colours on a white background and made of cut-out cloth—18. and 19. Police caps from 1776 to 1791.

20. Fusilier of the Colonel General's (1st) regiment (see fig 1 in series D)—21. Fusilier of the King's (23rd) regiment (see fig 1 of series A). The two types of helmet shown here were worn only by the fusiliers of these two regiments. The colonel's company had a white plume, and the ordinary regiments a black one.

Insignia of rank: a. commanding officer—b. second in command—c. other commanding officers—The lieutenant colonel had a single epaulet on the left in the style of a—d. major—e. captain—f. captain (second in charge)—g. replacement captain—h. first lieutenant—i. second lieutenant—j. lieutenant—k. replacement lieutenant—l. flag-bearer—m. sergeant adjutant—n. gentleman soldier (worn on each shoulder). These epaulets were worn on the left shoulder with, on the right shoulder, a matching epaulet, similar to a shoulder strap. When the uniform buttons were silver the rank insignia was silver not gold.

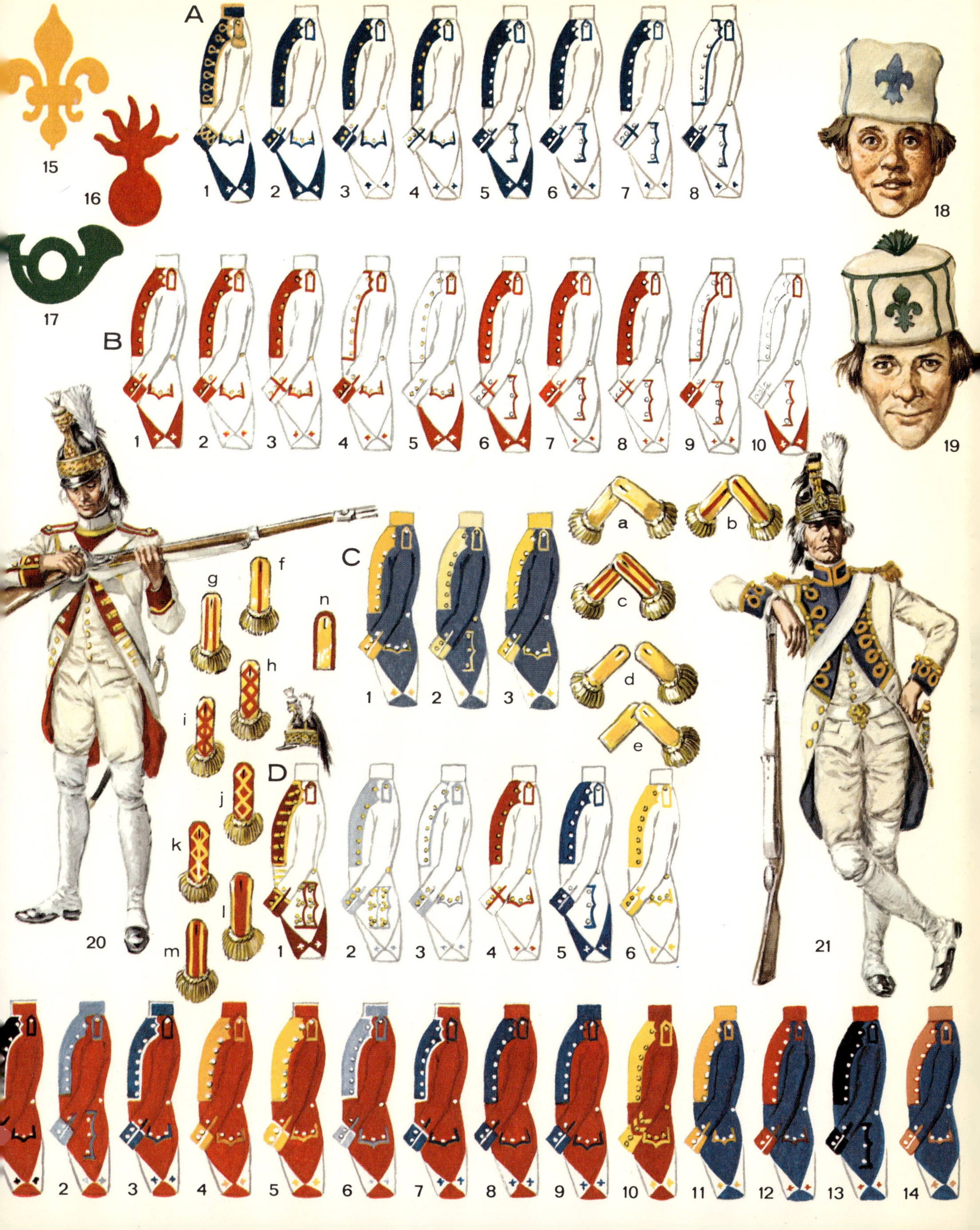

A
1 2 3 4 5 6 7 8
15
16
17
18
19
B
1 2 3 4 5 6 7 8 9 10
C
1 2 3
a b c d e
f g h i j k l m n
D
1 2 3 4 5 6
20
21
2 3 4 5 6 7 8 9 10 11 12 13 14

Fraters (Barbers-bleeders): each shaved only the men in their company. Their rank was marked by a little buttonhole in the shape of a goosefoot outlined with a woollen braid 7mm wide in blue on white cuffs, and white on other colours. They were abolished in 1782.

1786

Adjutants: one epaulet of flame silk on the left and two braids of the same colour as the buttons placed diagonally.
Sergeant-majors: two silver braids placed diagonally on the forearm.
Quartermasters: two braids as above, but on the arm.
Sergeants: a single silver braid placed diagonally on the forearm. The silver braid was made more visible by a row of piping in the regimental colour.
Corporals: two braids like those of the sergeant-n ajor, but blue on a white uniform and white on others.
Appointes (Lance-Corporals): one braid of blue wool or white thread positioned as for the sergeants.
Gentlemen-soldiers: two shoulder straps with 34mm wide gold or silver braid lined and piped with the regimental colour for the fusiliers, with scarlet for the grenadiers and with green for the light infantry.
Re-enlisted soldiers: on the top of the sleeve they had a stripe or a double stripe 2.25cm wide, in blue wool or white thread (instigated in 1771). Each of these stripes represented eight years' re-enlisted service. The re-enlisted lance-corporals and sergeants wore this ranking in blue braid 12.5mm wide on the jacket, not the coat.

FRANCE, INFANTRY
STATUTE AND TEMPORARY REGULATIONS OF 1791

A. First series, first group: 1. Colonel General—2. Picardy—3. Piedmont—7. Champagne—8. Austrasie—9. Normandy. The second group (not shown in the illustrations) had the same distinctions as the above regiments, differing only in having white buttons. The same is true of the other series—For the first and second group of the seven series, each of the first three regiments had horizontal pockets, while the last three had vertical ones. The only exceptions to this rule were the 1st regiment, the former Colonel General, and the 2nd, the former Picardy, which kept horizontal pockets with the typical goosefoot shaped buttonholes.
Second group: 4. Provence—5. Navarre—6. Armagnac—10. Neustrie—11. The Navy—12. Auxerrois.
B. Second series, first group: 13. Bourbonnais—14. Forez—15. Béarn—19. Flanders—20. Cambrésis—21. Guyenne.
Second group: 16. Agénois—17. Auvergne—18. Royal Auvergne—22. Viennese—23. Royal—24. Brie.
C. Third series, first group: 25. Poitou—26. Bresse—27. Lyonnais—31. Aunis—32. Bassigny—33. Touraine.
Second group: 28. Du Maine—29. Dauphin—30. Du Perche—34. Angoulême—35. Aquitaine—36. Anjou.
D. Fourth series, first group: 37. Turenne—38. Dauphiné—39. Ile-de-France—43. Royal Vessels—44. Orléans—45. La Couronne.
Second Group: 40. Soissonnais—41. The Queen's—42. Limousin—46. Brittany—47. Lorraine—48. Artois.
E. Fifth series, first group: 49. Vintimille—50. Hainaut—51. La Sarre—56. Bourbon—57. Beauvaisis—58. Rouergue.
Second group: 52. La Fère—54. Royal Roussillon—55. Condé—59. Burgundy—60. Royal Navy—61. Vermandois.
F. Sixth series, first group: 67. Languedoc—68. Beauce—70. Médoc—74. Beaujolais—75. Monsieur—78. Penthièvre.
Second group: 71. Vivarais—72. Vexin—73. Royal Comtois—79. Bourbonnais—80. Angoumois—81. Conti.
G. Seventh series, first group: 82. Saintonge—83. Foix—84. Rohan (uniform with crosswise pockets only).
Second group: 90. Chartres—91. Barrois—93. Enghien.

H. Officer—I. Fusilier. On parade, the helmet had a white plume with its top dyed in the regimental colour. On the left is a detail of the bayonet cover—J. Drummer. His lapels, collar and cuffs are in the regimental colour, sky blue, showing that he belongs to the 4th series and his buttons are yellow, showing that he belongs to the first group. The number of his regiment could be deduced by looking at the pockets from the side. If horizontal, he belonged to the 37th or the former Turenne regiment. If vertical, he belonged to the 43rd or former Royal Vessels regiment—K. Grenadier's bearskin. On the left, a detail of the base—L. Peaked bearskin. It was seldom worn like this.

2 3 7 8 9
B
13 14 15 19 20 21
26 27 31 32 33
D
37 38 39 43 44 45
50 51 56 57 58
F
67 68 70 74 75 78
H
G
82 83 84
I
K
L
J
L. & F. FUNCKEN.

1791

As above, except that the quartermasters became corporals and wore corresponding braiding with a narrow extra braiding above the elbow.

Officers

For a long time officers were distinguished by the rich embroidery on their uniforms and the fine quality of the cloth. The most noticeable and the most 'military' sign of their status was a crescent-shaped piece of metal. It had originally been a piece of armour worn to protect the gap where the helmet and the breastplate joined. It became a purely decorative symbol and was made in gold for the French and Irish, silver for the Swiss and burnished steel for the Germans.

Many of the officers intensely disliked obeying the order to wear the same uniform as their men. The rigid and precise terms used in the statutes of 1729 and 1737 are enough to indicate the reluctance of many of the officers to follow the regulations.

Distinguishing one rank from another was impossible and one had to be content with recognizing the various officers and knowing their ranks. This was not resolved until the statute of 18 December 1762 in which epaulets[1] were introduced.

[1] These epaulets were very unpopular and were given the nickname 'Choiseul's tatters' after the Minister of War, Choiseul, who introduced them.

FRANCE—INFANTRY
STATUTE AND TEMPORARY REGULATIONS OF 1791 II AND 1792

Foreign Regiments: German Regiments 53. Alsace—62. Salm-Salm—77. La Marck—89. Royal-Swedish—94. Hessen-Darmstadt—96. Nassau—98. Bouillon—99. Royal Deux-Ponts—101. Royal Liégeois. Irish regiments: 87. Dillon—88. Berwick—92. Walsh. Dillon, Berwick and Walsh are also quoted as having horizontal pocket and yellow buttons. Swiss Regiments: 63. Ernest—64. Salis-Samade—65. Sonnenberg—66. Castellas—69. Vigier—76. Lullin de Châteauvieux—85. Diesbach—86. Courten—95. Salis-Grisons—97. Steiner—100. Diesbach.
From 1 January 1791, all the regiments named above, including those on the preceding page were distinguished only by the number of the rank they occupied which corresponds to our numbering.

The new classification of the infantry of the line on 15 January 1792 led to other modifications.
Regiments 49 to 60 adopt crimson as their colour.
Regiments 61, 62, 67, 68, 70 to 75, 77 and 78 have scarlet.
Regiments 79 to 84 and 87 to 92 royal blue.
Regiments 93, 94, 96, 98, 99, 101 to 107 dark green and regiments 108 to 111 bright green.
The foreign regiments nevertheless also formed part of the French Infantry. Alsace (53rd), Salm-Salm (62nd), La Marck (77th), Dillon (87th), Berwick (88th), Royal Swedish (89th), Walsh (92nd), Royal Hessen-Darmstadt (94th), Nassau (96th), Bouillon (98th), Royal Deux-Ponts (99th) and the Royal-Liégeois (101st) consequently wore a white uniform with the colours as given earlier. (Temporary Regulation of 15 January 1792.)
As one can see, the Swiss regiments are not mentioned here; they had in fact been disbanded before the new modifications took place.

1. *Chasseur* or light infantry man before 1786. His hair here is tied in a knot but from 1789 onward it had to be worn in a plait.—2. Fusilier of a foreign regiment before 1789.—3. Fusilier in 1786. The ordinary soldiers carried the bayonet fastened to the strap of the powder flask as shown in the drawing on the left, whereas the corporal and the sergeant still carried this weapon by the side of the sabre (see fig 1)—4. Sergeant major of the grenadiers in 1791. In order to make the braiding stand out they were edged with the regimental colour. The sergeants had a similar braid on each sleeve. Notice that although they are still wearing the sabre strap, the sergeant is wearing his bayonet hooked to the strap for the powder flask. Moustaches were not allowed for grenadiers.—5. Corporal of the fusiliers in 1791. While fur-crested helmets were still being made, the hat was worn. This had to be tilted down over the right eye, with the point not in the centre but over the left eye. The helmet and the cap were worn perfectly horizontally.

62
77
89
94
96
98
99
101
87
88
92
63
64
65
66
69
76
85
86
95
97
100
1
2
3
4
5
L.&F.Funcken

Colonel: two gold or silver epaulets heavily fringed and with corded knots.
Lieutenant Colonel: a single epaulet in the same style as colonels, on the left shoulder.
Major: two gold or silver epaulets with single fringes.
Assistant Major: a single epaulet in the same style as that of major, worn on the left shoulder.
Captain: the same as the assistant major.
Lieutenant: One silk epaulet divided into squares in yellow or white depending on the colour of the buttons.
Second Lieutenant: one silk epaulet in yellow or white depending, on the colour of the buttons.
Flag-bearer: one yellow or white epaulet edged with gold or silver.
The single fringes on the epaulets of the lieutenants and second lieutenants were mixed with silk.

From about 1767 regimental colours were used for the silk parts of the epaulets, while the standard-bearer and the quartermasters adopted silk epaulets of blue or the regimental colour, but finally they all became flame coloured. The muslin and lace frills which had been worn at the neck and wrists up to 1775, were now strictly forbidden. At the same time, the officers' uniform, although made in better quality cloth, became identical to that of the ordinary soldier. For about ten years frock coats had been used for undress uniform. These had to be the same colour as the coat but this recommendation was not observed by everyone.

In 1786 there was no change made to the uniform except that it was supplemented by an overcoat, in the same colour as the coat and bedecked with a little circular cape edged with a 27mm braid, the colour of which matched the buttons.

As the epaulets are illustrated it is sufficient to give only a few details.
Camp Commander: The epaulets were 54mm wide and the fringe 54mm long.
Army Brigadier: Any kind of embroidery or decoration was forbidden but a superior officers holding the office of Brigadier wore epaulets of their own rank with an additional star embroidered in gold or silver to contrast with the colour of the epaulet which still matched the buttons.
Second Camp Commander: The flame silk cord was doubled in 1779

FRANCE—CHASSEURS À PIED
(THE LIGHT INFANTRY) 1784–1791

8 May, 8 August 1784: 1. Alpine Chasseur—2. Pyrénées Chasseurs—3. Vosges Chasseurs—4. Cévennes Chasseurs—5. Gévaudan Chasseurs—6. Ardennes Chasseurs.

1 October 1786: 7. Alpine Chasseurs—8. Pyrénées Chasseurs—9. Vosges Chasseurs—10. Cévennes Chasseurs—11. Gévaudan Chasseurs—12. Ardennes Chasseurs.

17 March 1788: Chasseurs from: 13. Royal Provence—14. Royal Dauphiné—15. Royal Corsican—16. Corsican—17. Cantabres—18. Brittany—19. Auvergne—20. Vosges—21. Cévennes—22. Gévaudan—23. Ardennes—24. Roussillon.

1 April 1791: Chasseurs à Pied (white jacket, breeches and fur-crested helmet)—25. 1st Battalion—26. 2nd Battalion—27. 3rd Battalion—28. 4th Battalion—29. 5th Battalion—30. 6th Battalion—31. 7th Battalion—32. 8th Battalion—33. 9th Battalion—34. 10th Battalion—35. 11th Battalion—36. 12th Battalion—37. 13th Battalion—38. 14th Battalion.

39. Officer in 1788. Notice the 'English' boots—40. Chasseur in 1788. He is wearing gaiters made in the shape of 'hussar' boots—41. and 42. Views of both sides of the infantry helmet which replaced the hat from March 1788. The tricolour cockade replaced the white cockade in 1790.

1
2
3
4
5
6
7
8
9
10
11
12
13
14
15
16
17
18
19
20
21
22
23
24
25
26
27
28
29
30
31
32
33
34
35
36
37
38
39
40
41
42

Second Captain: Cord doubled in 1779
Lieutenant and Second Lieutenant: The fringe on the epaulets was in gold or silver mixed with flame coloured silk.

The Hats

The officers hats were at first decorated with both gold and silver braid but after 1775 only silver was used. In 1786 the hats were edged with 11.25mm black silk braid. They had to be the same size as the troops hats and decorated in an identical fashion. The cockade made of white bombasine measured 94.71mm wide.

Over the crown of the hat, made of goatskin, the regiment colour was placed. The crowns of the staff officers hats were white. No kind of feather or plume was allowed.

FRANCE, INFANTRY AND DRUMMERS
(pages 88 and 89)

1. Drummer of the Colonel General regiment in 1786—2. Drummer of the Périgord regiment in 1767—3. Drummer of a royal regiment in 1737. The drum on the ground belongs to fig 3. The drums for figs 1 and 2 were made of copper with the number 67 on it and blue circles representing the Périgord regiment, without decoration and with white circles for the Colonel General regiment (according to Noirmont and Marbot)—4. Drummer of the Navy in 1772—5. Drum major of the Vexin regiment in 1772—6. Grenadier sergeant of the Dauphin regiment in 1724. He is carrying, by special privilege, one of the artillery forks captured from the Austrians at the siege of Mons in 1691. These forks were still carried by sergeants of the regiment during the Empire, a tradition inherited from the Dauphin regiment—7. Drummer of the King's regiment circa 1720—8. Drummer of the Lyonnais regiment wearing the Villeroy livery, circa 1720—9. Drummer from the type of regiment which wore the royal livery such as the Royal, Dauphin and Anjou regiments and any regiment bearing the name of a province around 1720. Below: detail of the braiding on the 'undress livery'. Doubled and then separated by the small braid shown on the right, it became the decoration for dress livery as is the case in fig 9—10. Drum major of the de Courten Swiss regiment (taken from a very beautiful de Rigo illustration)—11. Grenadier carpenter of the Navarre regiment in 1775—12. Soldier of the Artois regiment in 1775. He is wearing the jacket. Notice the wide opening under the arms which facilitated movement when this jacket was worn, which was nearly all the time.

Evolution of the uniform: A. Dauphin regiment in 1720—B. Dauphin regiment in 1755—C. The Vierzet Liégeois regiment with the coat completely fastened in 1767—D. Alsace (German regiment) in 1764—E. Courten (Swiss regiment) in 1767—F. Fusilier of the Flanders regiment, 1771 to 1775—G. Neustrie regiment in 1779. These drawings were largely inspired by a remarkable study by Rigo of the evolution of French Infantry uniforms.

The Chasseurs à Pied (Light Infantry)

The first *Chasseurs*, a mixed corps of foot soldiers and cavalry, attached to the Hussars, will be dealt with in the chapter on the cavalry, in Volume 2.

On 8 May 1784, six battalions and four companies were organized and each attached to one of the six regiments of *chasseurs à cheval*, (the mounted chasseurs).

On 17 March 1788, the Royal Italian, Royal Corsican and Montreal regiments were re-formed in the following way:
The 1st Royal Italian battalion became the Royal Provence Chasseurs. The 2nd Royal Italian battalion became the Royal Dauphiné Chasseurs. The remainder formed the core of the recently formed Royal Roussillon battalion. The 1st Royal Corsican battalion became the Royal Corsican Chasseurs. The 2nd Royal Corsican battalion became the Corsican Chasseurs. The remainder completed the Roussillon Chasseurs and the Cantabres Chasseurs. The Montreal regiment became the Cantabres Chasseurs.

At the same time, the older battalions of Chasseurs attached to the cavalry, were removed and reorganized into the new battalions as shown opposite. Each battalion had four companies and 108 men.

It was decreed on 1 April 1791 that they should in future be designated only by their number.

Royal Provence Chasseurs	from 1st Royal Italian battalion	1
Royal Dauphiné Chasseurs	from 2nd Royal Italian battalion	2
Royal Corsican Chasseurs	from 1st Royal Corsican battalion	3
Corsican Chasseurs	from 2nd Royal Corsican battalion	4
Cantabres Chasseurs	from Montreal and the remainder of the Royal Corsican	5
Breton Chasseurs	from the Alpine Regiment of 1786	6
Auvergne Chasseurs	from the Pyrénées Regiment of 1786	7
Vosges Chasseurs		8
Cévennes Chasseurs		9
Gévaudan Chasseurs		10
Ardennes Chasseurs		11
Roussillon Chasseurs	from the remainder of the Royal Italian and Royal Corsican regiments	12

A
B
C
D
E
F
11
12
2
1
3
4
5

G
10
6
7
8
9

THE BRITISH INFANTRY

In England soldiers' dress did not become a real uniform on a large scale until the Civil War, when the 'New Model Army' was organized in 1645 by Cromwell, and later fought the armies of Charles I at Naseby.[1]

Red had generally been the traditional colour during this dramatic period of change. The reason for this choice was the fact that red cloth was so very cheap.

It was not until the Restoration and Charles II's accession to the throne that Britain created a regular standing army. Between 1660 and 1685 its size increased from five to nine regiments.

Corporal John

Queen Anne was the first English monarch to issue a proper statute for her army, which became the British army when England and Scotland were united to become Great Britain in 1707.

The number of British regiments at this time was considerably smaller than the French for obvious reasons. First, Great Britain had the advantage of a geographical position which protected the country against a surprise invasion. There was, therefore, no need to maintain a large army. Secondly, with a population of about five million, which was only a quarter of that of France, her old enemy, she would have found it difficult to raise an army on an equal scale.

Recruitment was not easy as the army was unpopular with many people at all levels of

1 Decisive battle fought 14 June 1645 at 100 km north-north-east of London.

INFANTRY AT THE BEGINNING OF THE 18th CENTURY

1. Sergeant of a royal regiment in 1712 — 2. Soldier of a regiment of the line in 1712. At this time scarlet and crimson were used simultaneously. In some regiments the officers and sergeants reserved scarlet clothes for themselves and left the crimson ones for the troops — 3. Officer of the 1st Regiment, the Royal Regiment of Foot, in 1739. This was the oldest of the Scottish regiments called to serve in England in 1662 and considered by some to be the oldest one in Britain — 4. Grenadier of the 3rd Foot (The Buffs) in 1726. The demi-griffon, wearing a crown and collar and armed with a hatchet, is always represented in black. It is nevertheless certain that the arms of the Wills family were a blue demi-griffon standing on a blue and silver wreath. In fact the decoration on the cap reproduced exactly the traditional embellishment of the tournament helmets: the knight's coat of arms in three dimensions resting on a sort of garland, a baron's coronet which was used for securing this high piece on the polished iron skull of the helmet — 5. Grenadier of the Queen's Regiment in 1727, previously called Princess of Wales Regiment in 1715. The arms of the Prince of Wales apply here to the Princess of Wales, whose title the regiment bore until she became Queen in 1727. It was the only regiment to carry the emblem of the lamb and not that of the white horse of the House of Hanover. It was also the only one to display the motto *Pristinae virtutis memor* (Who remembers his old value) reserved for the Queen — 6. Officer of an infantry regiment in 1710 — 7. Soldier of an infantry regiment in 1715 — 8. Grenadier of Fox's Marines in 1709, disbanded in 1713. The marine regiments were chiefly used as landing troops.

TALBOT INN
1
2
3
4
5
6
7
8
L. & F. FUNCKEN

society. Many recruits were enlisted from the poorer classes and a certain number were criminals who enlisted as an alternative to prison.

Parliament, mindful of the tragic events of the previous century, and regarding a standing army to be a constant threat to its freedom, was extremely cautious and authoritative in controlling the forces which fought on the Continent. Furthermore, in spite of the fact that on paper the army was 40,000 strong, only 18,000 British soldiers fought in the Grand Alliance against France.

The army was led by a soldier of genius, John Churchill, first Duke of Marlborough. We need not mention his ambivalent attitude towards James II and his successor William III, nor the devious stratagems which made him one of the most powerful men of the realm under Queen Anne.[1] We are only concerned here with the military career of the great Marlborough, a career which began in France, where Charles II sent him to fight the Dutch on the side of the French. The young Churchill, barely twenty-two years old, served boldly under Turenne. His bearing and excellent manners earned him the name of 'Bel Anglais', and to his soldiers he was known affectionately as Corporal John.

Colonel at twenty-eight, Brigadier-General at thirty-five, at thirty-nine he was Commander-in-Chief of the troops sent in aid of the Dutch,

1 These monarchs reigned respectively from 1685 to 1689, from 1689 to 1702 and from 1702 to 1714.

INFANTRY 1742 I (according to the famous *Clothing Book*)

A, B, C. 1st, 2nd and 3rd Regiments of Foot Guards forming the infantry of Household Troops or troops of the King's House. The 1st Regiment did not take the name of Grenadier Guards until after Waterloo, the 2nd was already known by the name of Coldstream Guards and the 3rd did not receive its official title of Scots Guards until 1877.

1. 1st or Royal Regiment of Foot — 2. 2nd or The Queen's Own Regiment of Foot — 3. 3rd Regiment later called The Buffs — 4. 4th or King's Own Regiment of Foot — 5. 5th Foot — 6. 6th Foot — 7. 7th or Royal Fusiliers — 8. 8th or The King's Regiment — 9. 9th Foot — 10. 10th Foot — 11. 11th Foot — 12. 12th Foot — 13. 13th Foot — 14. 14th Foot — 15. 15th Foot — 16. 16th Foot — 17. 17th Foot — 18. 18th or The Royal Irish Regiment — 19. 19th Foot — 20. 20th Foot — 21. 21st or Royal North British Fusiliers — 22. 22nd Foot — 23. 23rd or The Royal Welsh Fusiliers — 24. 24th Foot — 25. 25th or Edinburgh Regiment of Foot.

In the second volume of his impressive work *A History of the Uniforms of the British Army* the late Cecil C. P. Lawson gives the 8th Regiment the characteristics of our 9th, while his 9th shows those of our 8th. In his elaborate study of the same subject our deceased collaborator and friend, Viscount Charles de Partz de Courtrai, shared this view. However, basing our knowledge on the fact that the 8th Royal Regiment had blue trousers, and relying on the descriptive list provided by William Y. Carman in his excellent *British Military Uniforms from Contemporary Pictures*, we have reversed the pictures of the two regiments.

The latter author gives, moreover, a whole series of interpretations relating to the braid: 2nd Foot — *black* and yellow stripes; 7th or Royal Fusiliers — a red *zigzag*; 9th Foot — red zigzag *plus* a *yellow* line; 19th Foot — a *green* chain; 21st or North British Fusiliers — a *wavy* blue line and not a zigzag; 25th Foot — wavy *red* and *green* lines.

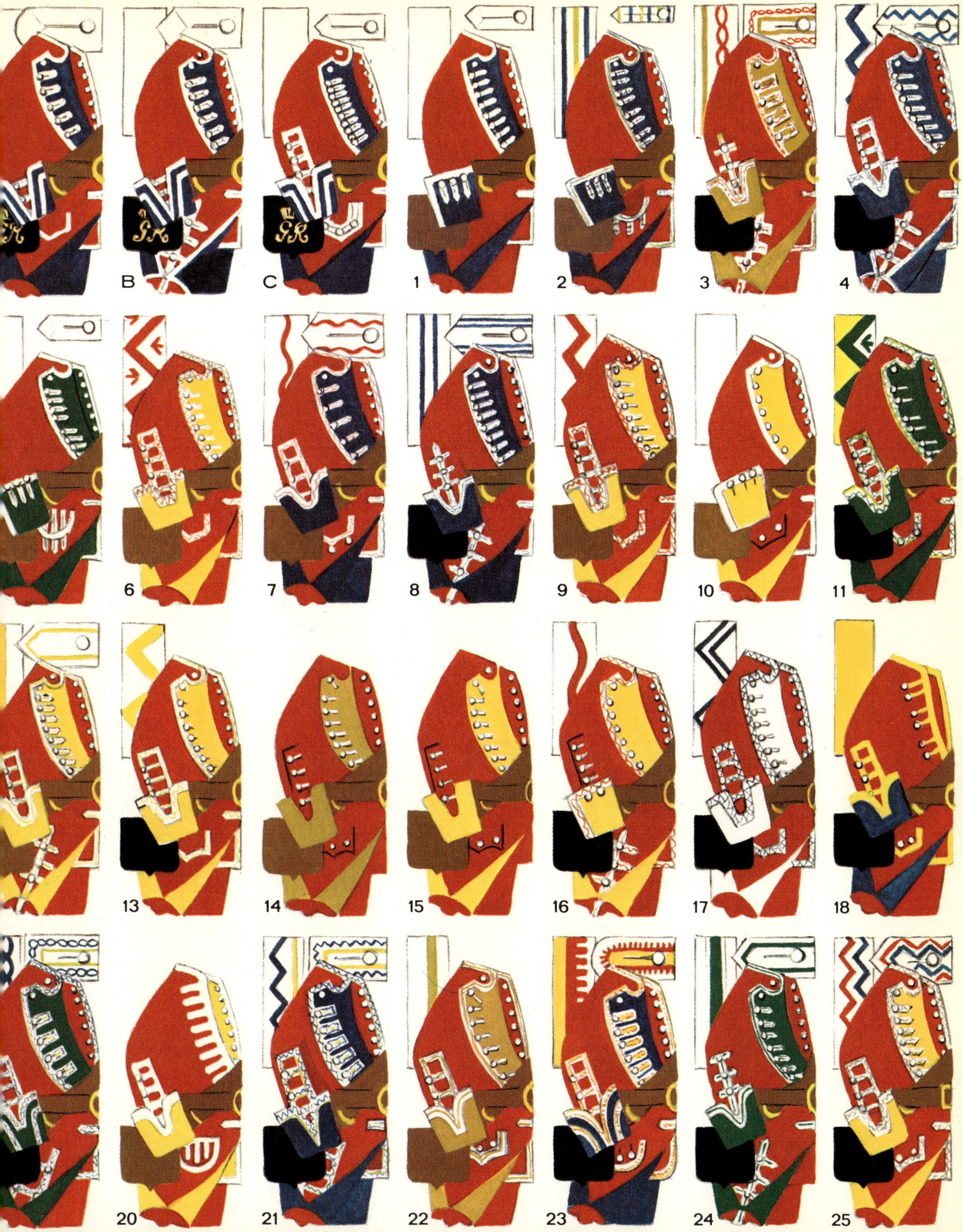
B
C
1
2
3
4
6
7
8
9
10
11
13
14
15
16
17
18
20
21
22
23
24
25

who were threatened by the French. In 1702, when the accession of Queen Anne coincided with the War of Spanish Succession. Marlborough achieved his ultimate ambition, and was appointed General at the head of the English army and Grand-Master of the artillery. He was soon put in command of the troops of the European allies as Captain-General of the combined armies of Great Britain, the United Dutch Provinces, Austria, Baden and several other minor German states. On the other side were France and Spain, who were joined in 1703 by Bavaria. This was a formidable opponent that was established in excellent strategic positions. And yet, for ten consecutive years Marlborough accumulated victories: Blenheim, Ramillies, Oudenaarde and Malplaquet, obtaining for Britain some of her most glorious triumphs.[1]

The happy strategian was showered with favours. Parliament presented him with the magnificent estate of Woodstock and the German Emperor bestowed on him the dignity of Prince of the Empire. Marlborough had become the 'God of the Alliance'.

By one of those strange caprices of fortune luck suddenly abandoned the illustrious soldier and gave way to an avalanche of attacks from the ministers of the new cabinet. Marlborough was forced to end the campaign he had led so brilliantly until then, under the humiliating control of a swarm of inspectors whose purpose was to expose his wrong doings. Recalled to London in 1712, he was accused of embezzlement, while the pamphlets of Prior, Saint-John and the celebrated Swift destroyed this former hero's popularity.[2]

Although opinions differ, we must mention that expressed by one of the most distinguished soldiers of our time, Lord Montgomery of Alamein, who, in his book *A History of Warfare*, declared that all the accusations against Marlborough were entirely false and that in fact the

1 Blenheim or Höchstädt (1704); on the Danube, between Ulm and Donauwörth. Ramillies (1706); in Belgium, at 20 km north of Namur, Oudenaarde (1708), also in Belgium, Malplaquet (1709), near Bavay, parish of Taisnières-sur-Hon.

2 Marlborough died at the age of seventy-two without ever having completely regained the respect of his fellow-countrymen. It was at his funeral that the practice of carrying muskets reversed in the air was inaugurated for the funerals of high-ranking officers.

INFANTRY 1742 II

26. 26th Foot — 27. 27th or Inniskilling Regiment — 28. 28th Foot — 29. 29th Foot — 30. 30th Foot — 31. 31st Foot — 32. 32nd Foot — 33. 33rd Foot — 34. 34th Foot — 35. 35th Foot — 36. 36th Foot — 37. 37th Foot — 38. 38th Foot — 39. 39th Foot — 40. 40th Foot — 40a. Invalids — 41. 41st Foot — 42. 42nd Foot (Scots) — 43. 43rd Foot or American Regiment, licensed in 1742. The place left vacant was allotted to the regiment that followed. The 44th therefore took the 43rd, in the same way as the following regiments from 45 to 50, who took the numbers 44 to 49 — 43a. 43rd new regiment, ex-44th — 44. 44th Foot ex-45th — 45. 45th Foot ex-46th — 46. 46th Foot ex-47th — 47. 47th new Foot ex-48th — 48. 48th Foot — 49. 49th Foot — 50. 50th Foot — 51. 1st Regiment of Marines. (For the others, see the following picture.)

Difference in the braid, after W. Y. Carman, op. cit.: 31st Foot — *yellow zigzag*; 32nd Foot — *green* lines and *red* chain; 37th Foot — *all yellow* and *absent on lapels*; 40th Foot — wavy *black* line and no green; 43rd new Foot — *black* stars; 49th Foot — *green* chain and *yellow* line.

27
28
29
30
31
32
34
35
36
37
38
39
40 a
41
42
43
43 a
44
46
47
48
49
50
51

great General did much to protect the army against the intrigues of profiteers.

The name of Marlborough was a familiar one on the Continent—more often than not as that of a mythical bully, a grotesque warrior . . . resulting in the famous song: *Malbrough s'en va-t-en guerre* (Marlborough goes to war). Curiously enough, this merry song, composed by a French soldier vexed by the insolent victories of this English devil, was not known in Paris before 1781 and it was at the court of Louis XVI that it became popular. More surprising still is the fact that the song had been copied from another, much older one, which was sung by the soldiers after the assassination of the Duc de Guise,[1] and which was itself a parody of a mournful romance of the Middle Ages sung by the Crusaders of Saint Louis![2]

The soldier

During the first ten years of the eighteenth century there suddenly arose from oblivion an army, whose glories at Crécy and Agincourt[3] had long been forgotten. The English soldier was proclaimed, as usual, 'the best soldier in the world' and he certainly did not owe this prestigious title to the skill of his Commander-in-Chief. He possessed all the necessary qualities: stamina, discipline and the skills of a crack shot. The fire of the British infantry was considered to be the most deadly in Europe.

There are few original documents relating to the uniform of the first decades of the eighteenth century. It is, nevertheless, possible to form some idea of the general appearance of the soldier, dressed as everywhere else in a uniform not unlike the civilian fashion but decorated with the traditional ornaments reserved for soldiers.

1 'The convoy of the Duc de Guise'.
2 Known in Spain by the name 'Song of Mambru'.
3 Battles fought in 1346 and 1415 respectively.

INFANTRY 1742 III

Marine regiments (cont.): 52. 2nd Regt — 53. 3rd Regt — 54. 4th Regt — 55. 5th Regt — 56. 6th Regt — 57. 7th Regt — 57a. *Idem*, according to Charles de Partz — 58. 8th Regt — 59. 9th Regt — 60. 10th Regt. All these regiments were disbanded in 1748.

Independent companies raised for service in the colonies: 61–68. 1st to 8th Company — 69. Soldier of the 2nd Foot Guards — 70. Soldier of the 13th Foot — 71. Officer of the 13th Foot.

53
54
55
56
57
57
a
59
60
61
62
63
64
66
68
69
70
71
L. & F.
FUNCKEN

These extras were not always found in the same profusion, and many a colonel dressed his soldiers in the most austere fashion, denying them even the smallest of ribbons on their hats and the emblems which adorned their heavy cartridge-boxes.

The practice of putting braid or lace on one side only of the uniform—namely, on that with the buttonholes—could be interpreted as an economy measure, but it applied also to the uniforms of regiments which were granted the title of 'Royal'. It seems that this asymmetry was favoured for a while.

The grenadiers

The grenadiers, who appeared around 1678, were from the beginning the elite of the regiment. Composed of the tallest and most courageous men, they were often used in much the same way as modern assault troops.

At this time the complicated movements necessary for the throwing of the grenade[1] made the adoption of a special headdress a necessary measure.

The grenadier had to carry his projectiles in his grenade-pouch, a big sling-bag with room for four to twelve grenades, depending on their size; he had to free the wick, which was protected by a small cardboard or wooden tube; take hold of the ignition wick in a special case fastened on his chest; blow on it to make it glow, and then apply it to the fuse of the grenade. Before the grenadier could throw his grenade, he had first to sling his musket across his shoulder, which meant that he could not wear the cumbersome three-cornered hat which was generally worn. A tall hat without any projecting brim was then chosen: from now on the cap and bearskin became the headdress of the elite troops. All these features, not forgetting the case with the ignition wick, which was useless after the grenade was thrown, made the grenadier one of the most picturesque figures of the eighteenth-century army. The front of the cap was at first decorated with

1 The grenade was a ball of metal, usually made of cast iron and filled with gunpowder.

INFANTRY 1742 IV

1. Soldier of the 36th Regiment, also called 'hat man' of the centre companies (hat companies), as opposed to the company of grenadiers, who wore the cap — 2. Soldier of the 23rd Regiment or Royal Welsh Fusiliers wearing the blue breeches reserved for royal regiments — 3. Grenadier of the 49th Regiment — 4. Soldier of the 6th Marine Regiment. The 9th Regiment also wore blue striped gaiters, which fitted loosely around the knees and were one of the characteristic aspects of the drawings of those days. The small leather straps at the end of the wide shoulder belt, which was worn across the chest, carried a pricker used to clear the touchhole at the breech which contained the charge and the ball, as well as a small brush for cleaning the pan after firing. (A detailed explanation of the functioning of flintlocks can be found on page 118, no. 72.)

5. English musket, called the 'long land musket', from the beginning of the eighteenth century. The term 'land' indicated a weapon used by land troops, as opposed to weapons used by the Navy or by the infantry troops of the marines. This weapon was more commonly known as a Brown Bess, and Bess was, according to some, a dimunitive of Elisabeth — a daring and romantic interpretation! The name was more likely derived from the word *Büchse* or from *Buss*, the names of muskets in Germany and in Holland, and imported by the Dutch troops in the service of King William III (1688–1702). This is the most plausible explanation, put forward by the British uniform expert W. Y. Carman in *A History of Firearms*. R. Held, in his *Age of Firearms*, assumes that brown owed its origin to the application of acid polish to the barrel, making it less shiny and more resistant to rust. This author nevertheless points out that such a practice was widespread and, besides, that the resulting brown colour did not last more than a few years of service and intensive polishing — 6. Detail of a Brown Bess dated 1727. The official stamp 'Tower' (Arsenal of the Tower of London) and also the crown and royal cipher GR (George Rex) relating to King George I can be seen quite clearly. The butt (a), which is very accentuated, is the most striking feature of the musket at that time — 7. Detail of the bayonet.

5
a
GR
6
1
2
3
4
7
L. & F. Funcken.

the arms of the Colonel of the regiment. This practice was abolished towards the middle of the century, when the arms were replaced by the royal cipher GR.

The fusiliers

The first regiment of fusiliers was created in 1685 from two independent companies which formed the garrison of the Tower of London. For this reason they were called The Tower Guards, then Our Royal Regiment of Fusiliers[1] or Our Ordnance Regiment under the command of the Master-General of Ordnance, who commanded all the artillery and its train and whose headquarters were in the Tower.

Composed of civilians recruited for the duration of the campaign, the artillery train had to have a military escort capable of defending her against the enemy and also of forcing, if necessary, the civilian drivers to confront the danger by resisting the temptation of running away at the first burst of fire.

The number of matchlock muskets in use was still considerable, even during the reign of William III (1689–1702). They made up half the firearms in use. The fusiliers were issued with a flintlock musket known as a fusil or fusee, light but costly. This weapon dispensed with the glowing match, thus reducing the dangers of accidental explosions among the stores of gunpowder.

Twelve companies strong at the start, plus one company of minors, the regiment ceased to be attached to the artillery about 1690, and at the same time lost its minors. It was renamed The 7th Regiment of Foot, Royal Fusiliers.

From 1695 the fusiliers wore the cap, according to a royal decree which forbade the wearing of this form of headdress by regiments which had adopted it without having the right to do so.

General issue of the flintlock to the whole infantry did not put an end to the title 'fusilier', which continued to be used by several units of

1 The original name has continued to exist until this day and the actual Royal Regiment of Fusiliers has its own regimental museum in the Tower of London.

INFANTRY 1750–1 I

A, B, C. 1st, 2nd and 3rd Foot Guards, making up the infantry of Household Troops — in other words the King's House.

1. 1st or Royal Regiment — 2. 2nd or Queen's Royal Regiment — 3. 3rd Regt or The Buffs. Formed in London in 1572 to help the Dutch in their struggle against Spain, this regiment was re-integrated in the English army in 1665, under the name of The Holland Regiment. Its distinctive colour, buff or camel, gave it its famous nickname — 4. 4th or King's Own Regiment — 5. 5th Regt — 6. 6th Regt — 7. 7th or Royal Fusiliers — 8. 8th or King's Regiment — 9. 9th Regt — 10. 10th Regt — 11. 11th Regt — 12. 12th Regt — 13. 13th Regt — 14. 14th Regt — 15. 15th Regt — 16. 16th Regt — 17. 17th Regt — 18. 18th Regt or Royal Irish — 19. 19th Regt — 20. 20th Regt — 21. 21st Regt or Royal North British Fusiliers — 22. 22nd Regt — 23. 23rd Regt or Royal Welsh Fusiliers — 24. 24th Regt — 25. 25th Regt.

B
C
1
2
3
4
6
7
8
9
10
11
13
14
15
16
17
18
20
21
22
23
24
25

the British infantry. Other regiments of fusiliers, created after the seventh one, enjoyed the same privilege.

In the middle of the eighteenth century the outline of the fusilier closely resembled that of the grenadier and, curiously enough, the grenadiers' ignition-wick case, which was identical to that of the old musketeers, was carried by the fusiliers.

The fusiliers were so much like the grenadiers that it was thought unnecessary for them to have a company of grenadiers, after the fashion of other regiments. Differentiation between these two classes of elite soldiers did not arise until 1768, when the fusiliers were given fur hats, which were not as tall as those of the grenadiers.

Headdress

The round felt hat of the previous century underwent a great change. The brims were turned up to make the three-cornered hat, called for some time a *ramillie* or *kevenhuller*, the latter name referring to a model of larger dimensions. It has often been suggested that the idea of turning up the brims of the hat was provoked by the difficulties that this imposing headdress caused while manipulating the musket, but it is far more likely that the hat, like the uniform, followed the steady change in civilian fashion. The poor esteem, not to say the contempt, held for the army at that time, did not in the least predispose the citizen, and even less the gentleman, to wear a hat like that of a soldier.

Later models, with the side corners becoming longer and longer, and with the front corner becoming decidedly less pronounced, gave rise to a two-cornered hat—a style known as the bicorne—which did not interfere with the movements involved in using the musket.[1] As always, fashion asserted itself. At the end of the century some troops wore a form of top hat. Early in the nineteenth century, however, the first purely military-style shako was introduced.

1 This type of headdress was called *retapé* (fluffed out or straightened) in France. When this word was applied to a hat, it meant to turn up the brim and press it against the crown.

INFANTRY 1750–1 II

26. 26th Regt — 27. 27th or Inniskilling Regiment — 28. 28th Regt — 29. 29th Regt — 30. 30th Regt — 31. 31st Regt — 32. 32nd Regt — 33. 33rd Regt — 34. 34th Regt — 34a. *Idem* with the wings in 1751 — 35. 35th Regt — 36. 36th Regt — 37. 37th Regt — 38. 38th Regt — 39. 39th Regt — 40. 40th Regt — 41. 41st Regt or Invalids — 42. 42nd Regt (Grenadier) — 43. 43rd Regt — 44. 44th Regt — 45. 45th Regt — 46. 46th Regt — 47. 47th Regt — 48. 48th Regt — 49. 49th Regt.

As can be observed, nineteen regiments wore wings on the shoulders. These embellishments had existed for a long time in some regiments, although their use had been forbidden during the year 1730. The non-conformists insisted on wearing them and their example became contagious. In 1752 an order was issued to fit wings to the coats of all the grenadiers in the British infantry. Whether it was given this ornament or not, the coat had a strap on the left shoulder, which was used to hold into position the belt, to which the cartridge-pouch was attached.

A. Tartan, or Government tartan, had to serve as a base for most of the Scottish regiments to come. Although much debated, this tartan is considered to be the one worn by the first regular Scottish troops in the service of the King. It is believed that the dark colours of the cloth gave rise to the name Black Watch given to the 42nd Regiment, a title which became official only in 1881. Since 1730, however, the first six independent companies raised by the Government five years earlier, and who in 1739 had to form the 43rd Regiment (later the 42nd), were also given the name of Black Watch. Certain Scottish authors think that this nickname could well have been, in the minds of the Scottish Jacobites, a mark of disapproval towards their fellow countrymen in the service of the English — B. Tartan of the 42nd Regiment, with the red line distinguishing the grenadiers, so it is thought.

6
27
28
29
30
31
32
3
34
34
a
35
36
37
38
9
40
41
42
43
44
45
46
47
48
49

The 1742 Clothing Book

It would be impossible to research, even briefly, into the history of British uniforms without referring to a book of great value known by several names: *1742 Book* (edited that year), *Clothing Book* or *Cumberland Book*—names far more suitable than the real title: *A Representation of the Clothing of His Majesty's Household and all the Forces upon the Establishments of Great Britain and Ireland.* It constitutes one of the earliest and almost complete sources relating to the uniforms of the infantry and cavalry regiments of that time. This extremely rare book has an extraordinary documentary value and is often considered in Continental Europe as a unique manuscript. It contains a number of copper-plate engravings. These appear to have been based on very good quality detailed drawings, although the engraver has lost some of their character leaving them a little lifeless. They are, nevertheless, of great charm and beauty. After first being printed in black, all the plates were coloured by hand. Two complete copies have survived and have been preserved with great care—one is in the British Museum, the other in the War Office Library. The royal collections of Windsor and the Prince Consort's Library seem to have only the plates relating to the cavalry. It has been said that a third complete set was presented to George Washington, but all trace of it has long since been lost.

In his delightful book *British Military Uniforms* James Laver mentions the existence of twenty-five reproductions of the original work, made by J.A.B. in 1893. Not all of them were coloured and they do not seem to have aroused much interest among the British specialists.

The best works on the subject are those by Cecil C. P. Lawson in the second volume of his *History of the Uniforms of the British Army*, (with diagrams by the great uniform expert William Y. Carman), and the recent study by Viscount Charles de Partz, published in the review of the Belgian Society for the Study of Uniforms and Costumes, with a beautiful set of engravings executed with great precision by Jacques Dubois.

Our most recent interpretation has largely been based on earlier works, with a few minor modifications, and reflects an opinion which on no account attempts to belittle or discredit those of the authors previously mentioned.

Who then was the person who instigated the elaboration of such an important subject? The British historians opt for the third son of George II, William Augustus, Duke of Cumberland, who was twenty years old in 1742. Colonel of the regiment of Coldstream Guards (2nd Foot Guards) at the age of nineteen, Major-General in 1742, he had fought bravely at Dettingen[1]

1 In Germany on the Main, west of Aschaffenburg.

INFANTRY 1750–1 III

1 and 2. Soldiers of the 6th and 2nd Regiments with complete equipment, or 'marching order' — 3. Soldier of the 7th Foot or Royal Fusiliers. In 1751 the decoration on the cap was modified by the discontinuance of the star and the enlargement of the garter and its central motif (the white rose and the red rose). Until about 1750 the braid was like that of the *Clothing Book* of 1742, and the pompom was white with a red base and a blue top — 4. Grenadier of 1st or Royal Regiment — 5. Grenadier of the 8th Foot, the King's Regiment. The wings became standard among the grenadiers from December 1752.

6. Detail of the tricorn. The front corner was distinctly worn over the left eye and was kept in place by a whalebone sewn on the brim of the hat — 7. Detail of the sword-frog. The sword was called a hanger. There was a great variety of swords in the Guards' collection. The swords had straight blades in the ordinary companies and curved blades in the grenadiers. These blades measured about 68 cm only in length — 8. Method of buttoning up the coat completely in winter. The ventral buttonholes disappeared almost completely underneath the belt (figs. 3, 4 and 5). The uniform shown belongs to the 12th Regiment — 9. Detail of the back with its false buttonholes without buttons and the braid peculiar to the 14th Regiment. 10. Detail and position of the vertical kind of pocket with a fishbone design — in this example with the braid of the 31st Regiment.

N.B. We are indebted to the great British uniform expert W. Y. Carman for the many details of these drawings, particularly with regard to the little known emblems on the caps of figs. 4 and 5.

L. & F. FUNCKEN
1
2
3
4
5
6
7
8
9
10

(23 June 1743) under his father, the last British sovereign to command his troops in battle in person.

In 1745 the young William Augustus, Commander-in-Chief of the Anglo-Hanoverian and Dutch troops, did not succeed in living up to the standards of his illustrious father and was defeated at Fontenoy by the Marshal de Saxe. Barely a year after this bitter defeat, the Duke of Cumberland encountered the Scottish Jacobite rebels on the Culloden moors[1] with Charles Edward Stuart, known as the Young Pretender, at their head. The battle, of little importance when taking into consideration the total strength of the army—9,000 British against 5,000 rebels—accounted for 1,000 dead among the rebels to every fifty redcoats. Its significance, however, was a different matter in view of the interests at stake and the tragic souvenirs that it called to mind. Cumberland, unquestionably victor, acquired for himself the name of 'Cumberland the butcher'—although atrocities had been committed on both sides—in addition to a supplementary yearly income of £25,000.

The military operations on the Continent in 1747 were only a series of defeats, from Lawfeld to the surrender of Kloster Zeven, which ten years later left the whole of Hanover to the French.[2]

Dismissed from the favour of George II and alarmed at the cold reception of his fellow countrymen, the Duke was forced to resign from his

1 At 8 km east of Inverness. This encounter was also called the battle of Drummossie.

2 Lawfeld, today called Laaffelt, is situated 3 km west of Maastricht. Kloster Zeven is a locality in the north of Germany near Hamburg.

HEADDRESSES OF GRENADIERS AND FUSILIERS IN THE MID-18th CENTURY

A. Cap of the Foot Guards towards 1740 representing a heraldic anomaly: the horse of the House of Hanover is on a blue background, although a red one would have been correct — B and C. Caps of the 1st and 2nd Foot Guards in 1751. The three infantry regiments of the Royal House have, in principle, the same caps. On the left, a detail of the central motif with the red cross of St George, symbol of England, superimposed on the Scottish cross of St Andrew. Observe that only the red cross of St Patrick, symbolizing Ireland, is required to make the British flag.

Infantry regiments: 1. 1st Regt or Royal Regiment of Foot — 2. 2nd Regt or The Queen's Royal Regiment — 3. 3rd Regt or The Buffs — 4. 4th Regt or The King's Own Regiment — 5. 5th Regt — 5a. *Idem*, seen from behind — 6. 6th Regt — 7. 7th Regt or Royal Fusiliers before 1751 — 7a. *Idem* in 1751 — 8. 8th Regt or The King's Regiment — 9. 9th Regt — 10. 10th Regt — 11. 11th Regt — 12. 12th Regt in 1750 — 12a. *Idem*, seen from behind — 13. 13th Regt — 14. 14th Regt — 15. 15th Regt — 16. 16th Regt — 17. 17th Regt — 18. 18th Regt or Royal Irish Regiment — 19. 19th Regt — 20. 20th Regt — 21. 21st Regt or Royal North British Fusiliers — 22. 22nd Regt — 23. 23rd Regt or Royal Welsh Fusiliers — 24. 24th Regt — 25. 25th Regt — 26. 26th Regt — 27. 27th Regt or Inniskilling Regiment — 28. 28th Regt — 29. 29th Regt — 30. 30th Regt — 31. 31st Regt — 32. 32nd Regt — 33. 33rd Regt — 33a. *Idem*, seen from behind — 34. 34th Regt — 34a. *Idem*, seen from behind — 35. 35th Regt — 36. 36th Regt — 37. 37th Regt — 38. 38th Regt — 39. 39th Regt — 40. 40th Regt — 41. Invalids Regiment. Although described in the *Royal Clothing Warrant* of 1751, this cap is hypothetical: not a single document in fact proves the existence of a company of grenadiers among these veterans, who were, for the most part, unfit to take strenuous exercise, and who were, besides, not meant to take part in active fighting. It is not, however, absolutely unreasonable to suppose that a company of grenadiers could have existed with a purely symbolic or honorary status — 42. 42nd Scots Regt — 43. 43rd Regt — 44. 44th Regt — 45. 45th Regt — 46. 46th Regt — 47. 47th Regt — 48. 48th Regt in 1750 — 48a. *Idem* in 1751 — 49. 49th Regt — 49a. *Idem*, seen from behind — 49b. *Idem*, variation.

The problem posed by the arrangement of the number on the back of the cap will without doubt never be completely explained. Before 1747, apparently, numbers were not shown. Later on, both arabic and roman numerals were used; the scarcity of caps now in existence does not assist us in deciphering the system which determined the choice of one type of number in preference to another. The grenade was not as widespread as is generally believed, and the 3rd Foot had only the roman number III. The 2nd Foot carried their number on the grenade; later, the 67th Regiment had a LXVII underneath; but most of the other caps which have come down to us bear an arabic number repeated on both sides of the symbolic grenade.

One will note that the front of the caps was of the distinctive colour of the regiment and adorned with the monogram or royal cipher GR for George Rex. The other, more elaborate emblems were reserved for the royal regiments and a few elite corps.

A B C 1 2 3 4 5 5a 6
7 7a 8 9 10 11 12 12a 13 14
15 16 17 18 19 20 21 22 23 24
25 26 27 28 29 30 31 32 33 33a
34 34a 35 36 37 38 39 40 41 42
43 44 45 46 47 48 48a 49 49a 49b
L. & F. FUNCKEN

military post and to retire to Windsor. During the reign of George III, owing to the inconstancy of the people, he regained his popularity. His death in 1765 was deeply felt.[1]

However, the contribution of Cumberland to military history could not be completely described without mentioning a second major element in the study of uniforms to which his name is attached: namely, the paintings he had commissioned about 1750 by a Swiss painter from Berne called David Morier. On his arrival in England in 1743 Morier was already well known for his painting of the battle of Dettingen, which can be seen in London's National Army Museum. This artist, then about forty-five years old, was commissioned by Cumberland to paint a grenadier from each of the regiments — an impressive idea, which constitutes a document of inestimable value in studying uniforms. The artist undoubtedly worked without models and without great enthusiasm: he gave his best only in his portraits of officers, but without reaching the standard of the great English masters. After exhibiting his works at the Society of Artists in 1760, Morier accumulated so many debts that he was put in the Fleet prison in 1769, where he died a miserable death the year after.

Walpole said of Cumberland, the artist's protector: 'He was as intent on establishing the form of spatterdashes and cockades as on taking a town.' Not only is this sentence unjust, but, moreover, who today would complain about the concrete proof of a love for uniforms which an unlucky warrior and a poor Swiss painter have bequeathed to us?

The reader will find much additional information in the monumental work by C. C. P. Lawson, mentioned above, from the beginnings until the Napoleonic wars. More concise, but remarkably clear and practical to consult, is the work by W. Y. Carman: *British Military Uniforms From Contemporary Pictures.* This presents in one authoritative volume the evolution of the military costume in Great Britain from Henry VII to this day. We must also mention the works of R. Monay Barnes on the same subject, very well illustrated by the author himself, and last but not least, the small booklets by Arthur Taylor in the *Discovery* series.

1 The custom of firing three salvos over soldiers' graves goes back to the accession of the Hanoverian monarchs. It is thought to have been imported by the German regiments. Each salvo represented one person of the Holy Trinity.

Drummers, fifers and musicians

Not often seen at the beginning of the century, drummers wore colours reversing those of their regiment. They wore the arms of their colonel on the back and had three-cornered hats. Their jackets and trousers were red. However, the drummers of the royal regiments wore the same uniform as the soldiers, and the uniforms of these corps were decorated with the royal arms.

Towards the middle of the century the fifers reappeared, first in the royal regiments, then, in 1747, in all the others. It was at that time,

DRUMMERS AND MUSICIANS OF THE INFANTRY REGIMENTS

1. Drummer of a royal regiment in 1751. The drummers and fifers of these units wore a red coat with blue as their distinctive colour, unlike the ordinary infantry regiments, who had as a background to their coat the distinctive colour of their regiment with lapels, cuffs and turn-ups in red — 2. Fifer of the 64th Regiment in 1745 — 3. Fifer of the 18th Regiment in 1758 — 4. Drummer of the 25th Regiment about 1768. The plentiful ornaments on the sleeves were abolished after that date. The Scottish origin of this regiment was to be found in the motto: *Nemo me impune lacessit* (No one harms me with impunity), written along the top edge of the badge on the fur cap. At the base was written XXV Regiment — 5. Fifer of the light company of the 7th Regiment of Royal Fusiliers in 1789 with the special cap of this company, also called 'the left flank'. Above the emblem of the star and the garter was written the traditional *Nec aspera terrent* (Difficulties be damned!).

In addition to their specific mission to brighten up the different phases of military life, the drummers were allocated the task of administering the punishment of the cat-o'-nine-tails. It is interesting to note that this barbaric punishment was still occasionally given in Britain until 1948 to convicts guilty of crimes accompanied by acts of violence.

2
3
1
4
5
DIEU
L. & F. FUNCKEN.

or perhaps later in 1751, that a new shape of hat seems to have been adopted by the fifers and drummers. It was a cap made of cloth with a lower crown than that of the grenadiers. As a special feature it had a kind of bag falling on one side ending in a tassel, in a manner not unlike the nightcaps worn by our ancestors. The front of the cap seemed to be just the place for a little decoration which, in the case of regiments without special insignia, was usually a motif of drums and flags.

The statute of 1751 formulated set rules for uniforms. The red uniform with the distinctive blue braid of the royal livery was given to the drummers and fifers of the royal regiments, while the others had uniforms in their characteristic colour with red lining and trimmings and also the regimental braid covering nearly all the seams. Long, full, false sleeves were one distinctive feature of the musicians, but they were not worn after 1768.

Bands of several drummers and one fifer quickly multiplied, but gradually more elaborate formations developed. The Guards inaugurated the first military orchestra, very modest at first of course, and around 1750 had two oboes, two clarinets, two basses and two horns. Their example was copied, despite the fact that the musicians were, for the greater part, an expense borne by the officers. It was for this reason that orchestras were usually limited to eight musicians, engaged, curiously enough, abroad, like the Hanoverian instrumentalists recruited in 1783 by the Duke of York, who allowed himself the extravagance of twenty-eight musicians. The expenses accepted by the colonels did have their rewards: the right to dress their musicians as they wished, a privilege which they exploited shamelessly.

Officers and non-commissioned officers

Officers

In Marlborough's time it was quite difficult t distinguish between the officers' ranks which were measured by the abundance of braid and decorations.

OFFICERS AND SERGEANTS OF THE INFANTRY

1. The Duke of Cumberland in dress uniform around 1750 At the age of twenty-nine, the youngest son of George I was, according to portraits of that time, abnormally stou — 2. Senior officer in 1756 — 3. General dressed in the uniform worn from 1767 to 1799. The Major-General hac buttonholes grouped in twos, the Lieutenant-General ir groups of three. The sash was knotted on the left side among officers of the infantry. Before 1772 the jacket, the breeche and coat-lining were all a buff colour — 4. Sergeant o the 11th Regiment in 1743 — 5. Sergeant of the 17th Regimen in 1777 — 6. Sergeant of the 30th Regiment in 1792. The pike replaced the halberd in 1792 — 7. Officer of the 4th Regiment in 1750. The coat is lined with blue — 8. Officer of the 1st or Royal Regiment (Scottish) in 1795. Note tha the braid on the hat was soon to be abolished for all the officers. In 1812 this regiment was to be called The Roya Scots — 9. Officer of the 7th Regiment or Royal Fusilier in 1791. Prince Edward, as Colonel of the regiment since 1784, introduced a number of special refinements to the uniforms of this unit — 10. Officer of the 15th Regimen in 1792. From 1791 all the gorgets were gilt, with a rosett made of ribbon in the distinctive colour at the corners — 11. Officer of the 2nd Regiment in 1799 and detail of a turn-up — 12. Officer with lapels buttoned up, 1799. From 1796 the bows or the tassels on the corners of the hat were gilt and crimson — 13. Officer of the 5th Battalion (ligh infantry) of the 60th or Royal American Regiment in 179 — 14. Officer of Manningham's Sharpshooters in 1800 Called the Rifle Corps, it became the 95th Foot in 1802 then the Rifle Brigade without a number, one year afte Waterloo. In order to look more like the cavalry, whose uniform they had adopted, the officers (like the soldiers of the new model light infantry often wore moustaches Another distinctive feature was the whistle, used for giving orders, which hung from the shoulder belt.

15. Epaulet of an officer of the grenadiers (60th Regiment around 1800 — 16. Epaulet of an officer of the light infantry around 1800.

1
2
3
4
5
6
7
8
9
10
11
12
13
14
15
16
F. FUNCKEN

Freedom of choice seems to have been granted to officers until 1740, although from time to time an officer could be seen in a uniform similar to that of his troops, but adorned with gilt or silver braid. He wore a crimson silk scarf from the right shoulder to the left hip, with the gorget and the shoulder-knot in gilt or silver to match the braid. The *Clothing Book* of 1742 does not give these details, but it is not unreasonable to assume that the gold was reserved for the royal regiments, and also for the 11th, 12th, 19th, 22nd, 25th, 27th, 32nd, 36th, 39th, 40th, Invalids and 42nd, while silver was given to all the others.

It is, in any case, the regulations of 1768 which allowed gold for the officers of the following regiments: 1st, 7th, 8th, 11th, 12th, 18th, 19th, 22nd, 25th, 27th, 32nd, 36th, 39th, 40th, 41st, 42nd, 48th, 49th, 51st, 53rd, 55th, 57th, 58th, 59th, 61st, 62nd, 63rd, 64th, 66th, 69th and 70th. Other regiments had silver braid or lace on their hats and clothes. The same regulations allowed two epaulets for the officers of the companies of grenadiers and only one, on the right, for the officers of the hat companies. The scarlet belt, tied round the waist, was worn by all.

Officers had carried the spontoon from 1700; it was abandoned in 1786 at the same time as the fusil, which they had carried since the middle of the century. It is interesting to note that they showed a marked preference for red trousers, while their troops wore blue ones.[1]

Non-commissioned officers

Sergeants carried the halberd from 1700 to 1792 when they were given spontoons not unlike those abandoned by the officers six years earlier. The sergeant of the light infantry continued to carry fusils.

During the reign of George II, probably around 1740, the sergeants adopted an extra badge which distinguished them when they were not carrying the halberd: it was a red woollen scarf in the centre of which, from 1768 onwards, was a stripe of their distinctive colour. The regiments with red as their distinctive colour had a white belt on their red scarf which was tied round the waist.

The only mark that distinguished corporals from ordinary soldiers was an epaulet in white cord attached to the right shoulder.

The uniform of the non-commissioned officers was made of the same cloth as that of the men. This plushy cloth of poor quality[2] was moreover dyed in a very mediocre way, and the red tint obtained by such a cheap process was in fact only a brick colour and much less striking than the shade one generally imagines. This practice continued until well after Waterloo. It was not until 1871 that the British foot-soldier appeared truly dressed in scarlet.

1 Certain royal regiments with blue trousers occasionally wore red trousers which were cut out of old uniforms.

2 During the first half of the century the greatcoat was worn one year only and then converted into a jacket.

The Scottish troops

The Scots have always had the military calling in their blood, and from time immemorial they have fought wars with tireless passion. Any pretext sufficed for this kind of activity—ranging from a quarrel with a neighbouring clan over a strip of land or the election or the dethronement of a king, to the raid on the herd and the harvest of the regions along the Anglo-Scottish border. Realizing that these exciting expeditions were not very lucrative and above all too sporadic, many hot-blooded Scots offered their services abroad, particularly in France.

The Lowland regiments

England also engaged a large number of these ferocious mercenaries from the Lowlands, and 1633 saw the birth of Sir John Hepburn's Regiment, which became The Royal Regiment of Foot in 1684, then The 1st or Royal Regiment in 1751. It was followed in 1642 by Argyll's Regiment, created by King Charles I in order to quell the Irish revolt, a task the Scots attacked with unusual savageness. Dissolved in 1650, this regiment was re-established ten years later under the name of The Footte Regiment of His Majestie's Lyffe Guards or The Scots Guards before becoming The 3rd Regiment of Foot Guards in 1712. Its record of active service was so extensive that it could almost retrace the history of British wars over three centuries!

Later came the Earl of Mar's Regiment, founded in 1678. It was called The Scots Fusiliers in 1685, classified as 21st Regiment in 1688, 21st or North British Fusiliers in 1707 and finally granted the title of 'Royal' in 1712.

The Earl of Leven's Regiment, raised in Edinburgh in 1689, apparently assembled 1,000 men in four hours! Leven's Regiment, or The Edinburgh Regiment, took the number 25 in 1751. And in 1782 the title 'The Sussex Regiment' was substituted for its old names.

The last of the five infantry regiments called up in the Lowlands, also in 1689, was the Cameronians, destined to uphold the cause of the Prince of Orange, the future King William III of England. It was given the number 26. It is interesting to observe that these companies had practically none of the traditional characteristics of the Scottish costumes. We call them assimilated regiments as they wore a purely English uniform, imposed on them by an official policy which tried to ignore the national pride anchored in the hearts of these mercenaries. In order to obliterate these feelings more thoroughly, care had to be taken to suppress typical Scottish clothing and armaments. This inflexible intolerance persisted until about 1881.

The Highlanders

When one considers the harsh treatment that was inflicted on the Lowland regiments, it is remarkable that the levy of a first regiment in the Highlands in 1739 introduced a surprisingly discordant note in the beautiful uniformity of the British troops. Clearly such an enormous concession was granted only because it was to be the sole method of enlisting the savage warriors of the interior.

A little worried and very curious, the King had, as a preliminary, insisted on meeting some of these 'barbarians' and had shown great satisfaction at their excellent performance of a sword dance.

The famous *Clothing Book* gives us a picture of a soldier of this first regiment numbered 43rd, then 42nd in 1749 after the dissolution of another regiment. Later on, the glorious regiment received the title of 'Royal' (42nd Royal Highland Regiment) in 1758 and formed, with its second battalion, the 73rd Perthshire Regiment in 1786.[1]

1 Not to be confused with the 73rd Regiment of Lord MacLeod's Highlanders called up in 1777 and renumbered 71st in 1786.

SCOTTISH TROOPS I

1–4. Scottish rebels. No special uniform was worn. The only emblem which made them recognizable was the white cockade. The Scottish irregulars who served under the English wore a black cockade. The classic arms were pistols made entirely of metal — including the butt — which, once fired usually at point-blank range, were thrown at the head of the enemy. The right hand was then free to draw the heavy sword, called the 'claybeg', universally misnamed the 'claymore', while the left hand seized the 'dirk', a sort of hunting knife, which at that time was supposed to measure the length of a forearm. The 'targaid', which was a small shield, round and flat, and often decorated with geometric figures in relief, was an important item in hand-to-hand fighting. The two-handed sword (fig. 2), called 'claidheam-mohr' (big sword), the real claymore, was given to particularly tall and strong men. Its blows were deadly. At the battle of Killiecrankie in 1689 these terrible arms cut to pieces a small Government army, composed, for the greater part, of Scots. The battlefield was covered with severed heads and limbs, severed with the same ease as a cane-stick cuts down wild flowers. There were bodies cut in half at the waist or even split from head to waist. Certainly, few regular troops could resist the devastating charge of the Highland warriors.

5. Grenadier of a Scottish regiment around 1715. His pouch bears the royal cipher of George I — 6. Grenadier of the Cameronians, 1709. Recruited in the Lowlands in 1689, this regiment had an organization which was both religious and military, inspired by a particularly active and austere Presbyterian sect called the Covenanters, a sect which was made illegal in 1660. The reprobates organized themselves into an armed force, made battle once, then again in 1680 under the leadership of a young preacher, Richard Cameron, only to be defeated a second time while losing their zealous leader whose head and hands were taken to the authorities in Edinburgh — an example of the uncouthness of the time. William of Nassau, who became King as William III in 1689, imposed the Presbyterian religion all over Scotland, gathering against him the faithful of the Episcopal Church who began to recruit an army. As a counter-measure the King decided to raise a regiment of Covenanters, who took the name of Cameron, their martyr — 7. Soldier of an independent company in 1730.

Principal clans who participated in the insurrection of 1745: 8. Cameron — 9. Farquharson — 10. Forbes — 11. Grant — 12. Macbean — 13. Macfie — 14. Mac Gillivray — 15. Mackinnon — 16. Mackintosh — 17. Maclachlan — 18. Maclaren — 19. Maclean of Duart — 20. Macnab — 21. Macpherson — 22. Murray of Athol — 23. Ogilvie.

In the contemporary painting relating to the battle of Culloden by David Morier the Scottish rebels do not wear any of these tartans. The artist had, apparently, worked from nature, thanks to his client the Duke of Cumberland who had provided him with prisoners as models. However — and this is surprising — the shields held by his models are convex, while it is absolutely certain they were completely flat! One must acknowledge, however, that the very few remains of tartans of that time which have been saved bear no resemblance to the modern tartans. We provide pictures of some of them, with all necessary reservation, in memory of the unhappy heroes of that time.

The background is inspired by the site of Glenfinnan whence the armies of Prince Charles Edward, 'Bonnie Prince Charlie', set out in 1745 to reclaim the throne of England and Scotland. This foolish venture ended in tragedy at the battle of Culloden, 16 April 1746 (cf. page 106).

1
2
3
4
5
6
7
8
9
10
11
12
13
14
15
16
17
18
19
20
21
22
23

The other principal regiments which followed were:

18th-century titles	*Modern titles*[1]
73rd Regt or MacLeod's Highlanders in 1777, 71st Regt in 1786 74th Regt or The 74th (Highland) Regiment of Foot in 1787	The Highland Light Infantry
72nd Regt—78th Highland in 1778, 72nd in 1786 78th Regt or Highland Regiment of Foot in 1793	The Seaforth Highlanders
75th Regt or Highland Regiment in 1787 92nd Regt—100th in 1794, 92nd in 1798	The Gordon Highlanders
79th Regt or Cameronian Volunteers in 1793	The Queen's Own Cameron Highlanders
91st Regt—98th in 1794, 91st in 1791 93rd Regt or Sutherland Regiment in 1800	The Argyll and Sutherland Highlanders

1 In 1881 the 'Cardwell System' reassembled some regiments in pairs (from 26th to 109th) making them 1st and 2nd battalions of a new regiment, and all the regiments were given the name of a geographical region or a title and were no longer referred to solely by a number.

SCOTTISH TROOPS II

1. Officer wearing the first uniform of the 43rd (then 42nd) Regiment nicknamed 'Am Freiceadan Dubh' or Black Watch, 1739 — 2. Officer of the same regiment in 1745 — 3. Soldier of the Black Watch in 1740 — 4. Soldier of the same regiment in 1742. The jacket worn longer than the coat was a typical Scottish fashion — 5. Corporal of the 43rd Regiment in 1743. His rank can be identified by the white shoulder-knot. The shield, which may come as a surprise here, was used in combat at least until 1745 in Flanders. Figs. 1, 2, 4, 5, 6 and 9 wear the 'breacan-an-feilidh', or belted plaid, while figs. 3, 8 and 11 wear the 'feilidh beag', or little kilt, also called 'philibeg'. It must be pointed out, regarding fig. 5, that certain prints of that time of considerable workmanship show the belted plaid worn in this unusual fashion. They also show the belts and straps as being of natural hide rather than the traditional black leather. Another interesting detail is that the wool used for the socks was dyed red with a kind of lichen called crotal geal or, scientifically, *Lecanora palescens*. This dye was supposed to prevent the feet getting too hot and blisters from forming during long marches — 6. Grenadier of the 42nd Regiment in 1751 — 7. Cap of the 77th Regiment in 1763. The tuft of feathers would soon become bigger until it reached the size of a large fur cap (see fig. 11). Figs. 6 and 9 have, on the contrary, real fur caps — 8. Officer of the centre company of the 73rd Regiment in 1777. The simple fusilier was almost identical, apart from the buttonholes edged with white braid set in red and, understandably, with the absence of the sash, the gorget and the epaulets replaced by simple shoulder-straps — 9. Officer of the grenadiers of the 73rd Highlanders in 1777. For the simple grenadier see notes on the previous fig., but with wings on the shoulders — 10. Soldier of the Cameronians in 1795. Since its creation in 1689 this regiment always exhibited all the characteristics of the British uniform. Reasons for this can be found in the text. The braid can be seen on the special page reserved for these details — 11. Soldier of the Gordon Highlanders (92nd Regiment) in 1798.

1
2
3
4
5
6
7
8
9
10
11
L. & F. FUNCKEN

The statute of 1768

The 'Royal Warrant' of 1768 marked out with great accuracy important distinctions and codified all the changes which had occurred in the uniforms since the legislation of 1751. Evidently, its effect was not immediately felt and old uniforms were still worn along with new ones. Red jackets and trousers were still favoured against the prescribed white ones.

The caps of embroidered cloth worn by the grenadiers and fusiliers did not surrender quickly to the new furry hat, particularly in the royal regiments who were proud of their own badges, more richly embroidered and flattering than the simple royal monogram of the other regiments. The men of the 7th Regiment of the Royal Fusiliers kept to their cherished cap at least until 1770.

Another innovation of the period was the adoption of numbered buttons, from one to seventy at that time. They were made of pewter for the troops, but in gilt or silver for the officers.

Affectation and the desire to be different from the other regiments led to the adornment of the simple stamped-on number. The Guards were among the first to introduce these embellishments which continued to spread.

According to the Royal Warrant, the buttons and braid of the hats and uniforms of officers were gilded in the following regiments: 1st, 2nd and 3rd Foot Guards, and infantry regiments 1st, 7th, 8th, 11th, 12th, 18th, 19th, 21st, 22nd, 23rd, 25th, 27th, 32nd, 36th, 39th, 40th, 41st, 42nd, 48th, 49th, 51st, 53rd, 55th, 57th, 58th, 64th, 66th, 69th and 70th. Silver was reserved for the other regiments.

Ordinary soldiers and sergeants had, apart from pewter buttons, lace with a white background. The lace was used for buttonholes at the lapels, in groups of four on the cuffs and on the pockets (false ones) and three on either side of the slit at the waist on the reverse of the dress-coat. The corporals replaced the white epaulet with a silk one on the right shoulder.

BRAID, BUTTONHOLES AND DISTINCTIVE COLOURS OF THE ROYAL ORDER OF 1768

1 to 70. From the 1st to the 70th Regiment (with the exception of the Guards). It is easy to read each scheme by referring to the black and white model at the foot of the group. A: braid. B: buttonhole. C: distinctive colour (collar, lapels, cuffs). D: jacket. E: breeches. As the shades of one and the same colour are not always easily distinguishable, we give the list as follows:

Buff (camel): 22nd Regt=pale buff; 62nd Regt=yellowish buff.

Yellow: 6th and 25th Regts=dark yellow; 10th, 28th and 34th Regts=bright yellow; 20th, 26th, 30th and 67th Regts=pale yellow; 13th Regt=*feuille morte* (a kind of yellow).

Red: 56th and 59th Regts=purple.

Green: 5th Regt=pale yellowish green; 11th and 49th Regts=bright green; 19th, 45th, 51st and 68th Regts=dark green; 55th Regt=dull green; 66th Regt=yellowish green; 24th and 69th Regts=clear olive green; 54th Regt=green, lined with yellow. White: 17th Regt=greyish white.

Orange: the 35th Regt, the only one to have this colour.

71. Cartridge in its wrapping of thick paper. The bullet always had a small bump on it, formed in the mould, and could be firmly fixed to the cartridge by means of a thread wound round this.

A: end to be ripped off with the teeth. B: portion of powder deposited in the pan for priming. C: charge of powder poured down the barrel. D: the ball is then slipped down the barrel at the same time as the cartridge paper wrapping. Everything is then rammed down with the ramrod — 72. Lock of a Brown Bess made by Grice in London in 1756. Lacking the mark of the Tower Arsenal, it bears, nevertheless, the crown and the royal cipher (George III at that time). The pan cover E lifts to reveal the pan F, used to hold the priming, which burns and flashes through the touchhole G (fig. 71 C and D). When the trigger is pressed, the cock is released and flies forward. The flint strikes the combined steel and pan cover E and pushes it clear of the pan so permitting the sparks produced by flint and steel to fall into the priming F. The priming burns and the flame passes through the touchhole G firing the main charge and so discharging the ball — 73. French infantry musket model 1728, with the butt called 'cow's foot' (1,593 m) — 74. French heavy musket de Stainville 1763 model (1,530 m) — 75. French infantry musket model 1777 made in Saint Etienne (1,520 m) — 76. Prussian infantry musket model 1796 (1,450 m). One look at the arms 73 and 76 shows the differences in appearance between the French make and the German one.

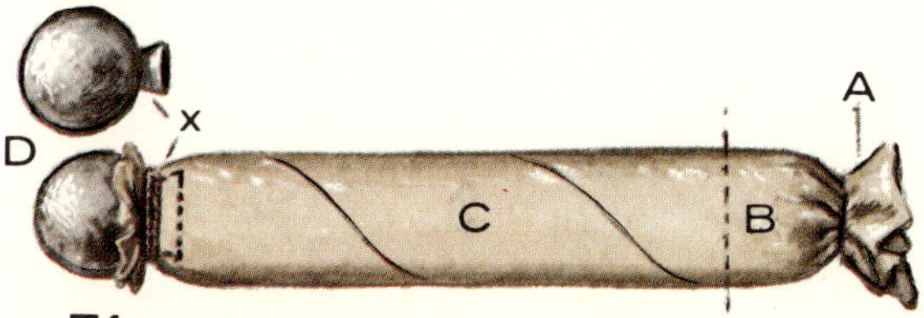

71

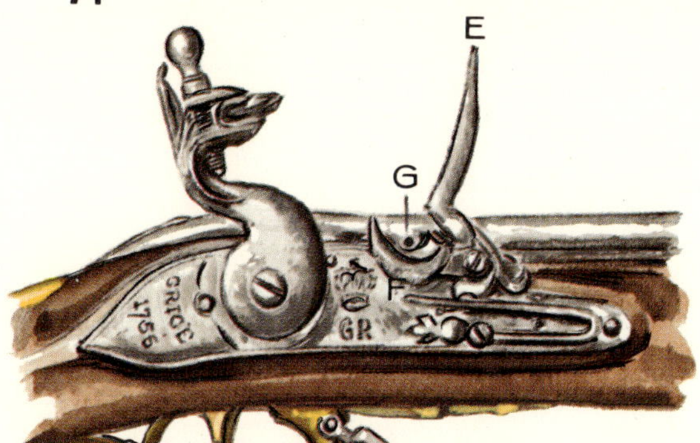

72

73 74 75

L. & F. FUNCKEN

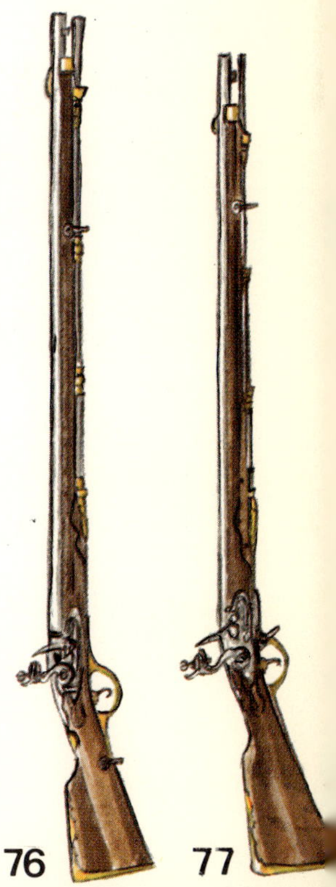

76 77

All other details relating to the distinctive colours of jackets, trousers and linings, including the buttonholes of each regiment, are shown on the previous page.

Standards

During the first decades of the eighteenth century the British army deployed a great number of standards which were very similar to those of the French. But the red cross of St George clearly distinguished them at a first glance from the adversary whose emblem was a white cross.

Each regiment had its royal standard in scarlet decorated with the initials of the sovereign surmounted by the royal crown. Colonels, majors and captains all had their own and designed them with as much imagination as their rank permitted. Apart from the personal arms of the colonels, the standards were adorned with an extraordinary variety of animals, symbols, monograms, flowers and pennants whose meanings and associations may never be explained.

This flood of colour and originality received a severe blow and was cut short in 1751 when a royal decree specified the previous instructions of 1743 and 1747 which had hitherto had little effect. From then on each regiment was entitled to have no more than two standards. The first, called the King's colour, which was the national standard, depicted the cross of St George and St Andrew together, a combination called the Great Union. The second emblem, the regimental colour or the regimental standard, had to have its background in the distinctive colour of the regiment and bear the Union in the top corner of the side attached to the staff. Where the main colour of the regiment was red or white, the regimental standard had to be that of St George—white with a large red cross over the entire length and width—and the Union in the upper section next to the staff. The regiments with black as their distinctive colour received the same standard but with the three empty sections black instead of white.

All regiments, except those which had been rewarded with special royal emblems, had in the centre of their standard a garland of roses and thistles encircling their number which was in roman characters.

The 3rd (The Buffs), 5th, 6th, 8th and 27th (Inniskilling's) regiments, who were endowed with royal emblems, placed them in the centre of their standard, instead of the garland described above, and put their number in the top corner of the side next to the staff.

COLOURS

1st or Royal Regiment — 2. 4th or King's Own Regiment, 1745 — 3. 8th or King's Regiment — 4. 10th Regiment in 1725. The use of the personal arms of the commanding Colonel was forbidden and they disappeared in 1751 — 5. 23rd or Royal Welsh Fusiliers in 1742 — 6. 27th or Inniskilling Regiment — 7. 12th Foot in 1768 — 8. 28th Foot in 1784. Note the influence of the decorative style in fashion at that time.

9. Ensign of the 1st Foot Guards with the colours of the Major of the 3rd battalion in 1776. The ensigns were not restricted to simply carrying the colours. They had to assimilate a whole series of very elaborate movements used in ceremonies. The picture represents the method of saluting a general at a military parade.

G-R
NEMO ME IMPUNE LACESSIT
1
2
GR
HONNI SOIT QUI MAL Y PENSE
Nec Aspera Terrent
3
VINCO MALUM BONO
4
ICH DIEN
5
9
L. & F. FUNCKEN
6
7
8
INNISKILLING
REGT XII
STABILIS
XXVIII REGT

The Foot Guards

At the time of the Restoration of the monarchy in 1660 the three regiments of the Royal Foot Guards were formed into a miniature personal army of Charles II.

The 1st Regiment

This corps was originally formed in Holland by the son of King Charles I and Henrietta of France, the future Charles II, who decided while in exile to give himself a regiment of Foot Guards. It was made up in 1656 from an existing regiment, called Wentworth's Regiment, which was re-named The Royal Regiment of Guards. When Charles II came to the throne in 1660, the regiment, having suffered many casualties, stayed in Holland and the sovereign created a second one which was recruited on British soil by Colonel John Russell. The Flanders regiment was repatriated in 1664 and amalgamated again under the name of The King's Royal Regiment of Guards, a title which was modified to The Regiment of Foot Guards in 1685. It was not until after Waterloo in 1815 that the regiment was granted the title of Grenadier Regiment of Foot Guards, nowadays simply shortened to Grenadier Guards.

The 2nd Regiment

The 2nd Regiment owes its origin to the curious personality George Monck, who accomplished the remarkable feat of serving in succession under Charles I, Oliver Cromwell, Richard Cromwell and Charles II. Colonel in the Royal army, captured in 1644, he was put at the head of a new regiment—The Monck's Regiment of Foot—by his conqueror Oliver Cromwell in 1650. With extraordinary flair, and favoured by the political confusion which was rife during the Government of Richard Cromwell, Monck managed to take advantage of the situation.

At the right moment he left his general quarters at Coldstream, a small Anglo-Scottish town, and led his regiment to London where he ensured law and order and the free election of a new Parliament which favoured the return of Charles II, who returned to the capital amidst general rejoicing. This skilful officer had succeeded with great expertise and, all consideration of his own private conception of loyalty set aside,[1] had spared his country from a second civil war.

Cromwell's old army was dissolved, including Monck's Regiment who ceremoniously laid down their arms after the parade at Tower Hill on the feast of St Valentine in 1661. Immediately after this gesture, the regiment picked up their

1 It would take a whole volume to retrace and try to explain objectively the career of this person.

FOOTGUARDS I

1. Soldier of the 2nd Regiment or The Scots Regiment of Foot Guards, 1710. In 1705 the laces were yellow. *Left*, detail of the decoration on the pouch — 2. Grenadier of the 1st Regiment in 1704 (Battle of Blenheim) — 3. Corporal of the grenadiers of the 1st Regiment; his rank is indicated by the shoulder-knot. The throwing of the grenade was regulated by traditional and detailed movements which were carefully executed. Here the soldier lights the slow match, which ignites the fuse of the grenade, which in turn explodes the projectile. The water-colours by Bernard Lens, dated 1735, are unusual as they do not show the indispensable fuse container in which the grenadier carried his fuse wick — 4. Sergeant of the 1st Regiment in 1745 — 5. Corporal of the grenadiers 3rd Regiment in 1751 with a match-case — 6. Fifer of the 1st Regiment in 1745 — 7. Grenadier of the 3rd Regiment in 1775. The front plate of the fur cap carries the royal arms flanked by the lion and the unicorn in white metal on a black background for the 1st, red for the 2nd, and in white metal entirely for the 3rd Regiment. Note here again the fuse container peculiar to the grenadiers; it was, however, purely ornamental — 8. Officer of the 1st Foot Guards in 1745 — 9. Officer of the 1st Regiment in town dress, 1745.

1
2
3
4
5
6
7
8
9

muskets and was reinstated under another name: The Lord General's Regiment of Foot Guards.[1]

On Monck's death it became The Coldstream Regiment of Foot Guards and it has kept the name of Coldstream Guards until this day.

The 3rd Regiment

In 1642 a Scottish regiment formed by the Duke of Argyll in 1639—Argyll's Regiment—was sent by Charles I to curb the troubles in Ireland. It stayed in Ulster until 1645, when it was recalled to Scotland to fight, this time, against the royalist troops of Montrose.[2] Sent back to Ulster in 1646, the regiment stayed there until 1650, the year following the execution of Charles I. Reduced to a very small effective force, it was then known by the name of Irish Companies. This small company returned to Scotland to serve under Charles II who had just landed there. Greatly reduced in numbers at the battle of Dunbar, the regiment was immediately reconstituted and re-named His Majestie's Foote Regiment of his Lyffe Guards and took part in the King's march on London. But this advance of the royalist troops was interrupted by the victory of Cromwell at Worcester in 1651. The survivors of the Lyffe Guards of Foot dispersed and the regiment ceased to exist. It reappeared during the Restoration and was garrisoned in Edinburgh and Dunbarton Castles. Enlarged by additional companies in 1662, it became The Scots Regiment of Foot Guards. Called back urgently to England to help in the suppression of Monmouth's revolt[3] in 1685, it was based in London the following year with the title of 3rd Regiment of Foot Guards. It was re-named The Scots Fusilier Guards in 1831 and obtained its final name of Scots Guards in 1877.

1686 marked the real date of the birth of the Foot Guards of the Royal Household. The Scots, who were the last to be formed, were given for this reason the nickname 'The Kiddies'. An irritating point was the fact that, although six years older than the 1st Regiment, The Coldstream Regiment, it was given second place by Charles II. Indignant but obedient, the frustrated regiment took for vengeance the motto: *Nulli secundus*, which means 'second to no one'. On parade days they always insisted on marching not immediately behind the 1st Regiment but well after the 3rd, showing their silent but obstinate protest.

1 Monck, who became Duke of Albemarle, owned the title of Lord General.

2 Royalist chief, the Marquis of Montrose (1612–50) led a diversionary expedition against Scotland at the beginning of the Civil War. He was hung in Edinburgh.

3 James Scott, Duke of Monmouth (1649–85), was pretender to the throne of James II. He died on the scaffold in the Tower of London.

FOOTGUARDS II

1. Drummer of the 1st Regiment in 1750 — 2. Drummer of the 3rd Regiment in 1798 — 3–5. Drummers of the 1st, 2nd and 3rd Foot Guards in 1789. The coats of arms shown are those of George I and George II. According to contemporary pictures, they still adorned the drummers of the 1st and 2nd Regiments of the Guards, despite the fact that the reigning sovereign was George III and that his coat of arms was slightly different. The 3rd Regiment (fig. 5) decorated its drummer with the star and cross of St Andrew — 6. Sergeant of the grenadiers of the 2nd Regiment in 1789. The motif on the cap and the silver braid were white for the ordinary grenadiers — 7. Grenadier of the 1st Regiment in 1789. Sergeants had the front plate and the braid in gold. The men of the 3rd Regiment wore a slightly more pointed fur cap (see fig. 5) with a front plate in white and gold — 8. Officer of the 2nd Regiment in 1790. Note the buttons on the lapels grouped in pairs, while they were equally spaced for the 1st Regiment and in groups of three for the 3rd. Apart from this small detail, the uniforms were identical — 9. Sergeant of the 1st Regiment in 1792. The sash of rank tied round the waist shows the white central line indicating the 1st Foot Guards; the 2nd Regiment had a sash completely in crimson and that of the 3rd was in crimson, white and blue. In the infantry regiments the central line was in the distinctive colour of the regiment, and this rule applied since 1768 — 10. Soldier of the 2nd Regiment in 1790.

1
2
3
4
5
6
7
8
9
10
F. FUNCKEN

The Light Infantry

It was during the war against the French in Canada around 1758 that the first troops of light infantry of the British army appeared. The altogether special nature of skirmishes in forests required the formation of specially trained troops, lightly dressed and armed.

The problem of the uniform was quickly solved: the tails of the traditional dress-coat were cut off to the level of the jacket, so that it would not get caught up in briars and low branches. The brightly coloured laces were also abandoned while 'wings' (crescent-like projections) were fixed to the shoulders, in order to hold up the equipment slings more effectively and also as a protection, no doubt, against blows on the shoulders by edged weapons.

The much lighter armament consisted of a shorter musket. The heavy and cumbersome cartridge-box was replaced by a small one, worn across the stomach, containing nine cartridges lined up in a row. In order to compensate for this poor provision of 'ready to use ammunition,'[1] the soldier carried a supply of gunpowder in a scooped-out cow's horn, which he often decorated artistically in his spare moments. Extra bullets were carried in a little bag hanging from a shoulder belt, or sometimes in two breast pockets made of leather which were sewn on the coat. These pockets were also used to carry the spare flints for the lock of the musket.

The bayonet was optional but the tomahawk was very much favoured. It was made in England and originally destined for trade with the Indians.

The hat was the most bizarre element of the equipment and was made up, at the start, from the three-cornered hat which had been cunningly cut away. Depending on circumstances and individual personality, Indian clothing was worn, resembling a type of riding outfit, delightfully unconventional.

The obvious usefulness of these troops led the authorities to create in 1770 a light company in each of the eighteen regiments serving in North America, and later in the whole body of the army. A hat called the 'tarleton' appeared in 1787 and was exactly like the crested helmets of the French infantry of 1791. The traditional red jacket disappeared in 1797.

1 For details concerning the cartridge see the illustration on page 119, no. 71.

LIGHT TROOPS

1. Light company of the 46th infantry of the line, 1778 — 2. Light company of the 5th infantry of the line, 1771 — 3. Light infantry in 1758. Note the lapels folded back on the stomach with small breast pockets added. These were used for holding the spare fuses and a few balls. The bayonet was often replaced by a tomahawk — 4. Light infantry in 1761 — 5. Officer about 1756. In North America deficiencies in leadership and the peculiar character of ambush war completely transformed the outline of the British soldier. The officers, almost wiped out by expert shooters, adopted a dress not unlike that of their men. Note the Indian leggings. The coat is cut at the waist and the hat, jockey style, is simply a smaller version of the tricorn — 6. Light company about 1765 — 7. Light company of the 2nd Regiment of Foot Guards in 1794. The regiments of the Guards did not have any light companies before 1792. The soldier wears breeches and gaiters in one piece, also used as overalls by the recruits.

8. Headdress of fig. 6. Towards 1765, when the light infantry had been more or less deserted, light companies were hastily formed. The skirt of the coat was shortened and the classic tricorn was cut down in order to obtain a suitable type of headdress — 9. Hat of fig. 7. This hat was also worn by the recruits of the Foot Guards during their training — 10. Headdress of fig. 1. This was a leather headdress reinforced with metal, as stipulated by the regulations. The picture opposite is one example amongst others of a very free interpretation of the regulations — 11 and 12. Headdress adopted by the 5th Regiment in 1771. Like the model of fig. 10 it protected the skull much better than the tricorn in single combat, in battles with edged weapons to which the light troops were often exposed. Note the number of the regiment on the central circle.

10
11
12
3
4
5
1
2
8
6
7
9
F. FUNCKEN

Evolution of the uniform

The hat

We have previously mentioned the appearance of the first three-cornered hat worn by the ordinary soldier as shown by illustrations of that time—with the front corner above the left eye. We have provided a drawing of it, seen from above,[1] but it occurred to us afterwards that the representations of the time, showing the front horn worn slightly to the left, could just as well suggest that the whole hat was worn a little sideways, in order to avoid the left corner getting in the way of the musket. As no authentic hats have been sufficiently well preserved for us to examine, we find it impossible to support this supposition. We must however not forget that the officers, who sometimes carried a fusil, wore the front corner at right angles to the centre of the face. The cockades of black cloth were replaced by leather ones in about 1790.

The cap

The officers of the grenadiers and fusiliers wore caps like their men, but they were more elaborately decorated.

Hair

Worn loose at the beginning of the century, the hair was later cut on the temples (or rather on the face) and on the neck, and fixed in plaits on top of the head. This curious arrangement gave the impression that the hair, when covered by the hat, was cut short.

In 1750 curls on the temples were allowed, while the rest of the hair was plaited. The pigtail or *queue* obtained that way was folded over twice, held in position under the hat, or held together with a fancy ribbon. To make a pigtail one had simply to gather one's hair together and tie a ribbon round it. No doubt after 1760 one or other of these methods was practised.

Wigs were unfashionable around 1710, except in the case of bald people, because the new, less voluminous hairstyle could easily be achieved with the natural hair. But as compensation it was common to powder the hair—a practice which, for ordinary soldiers, was approved only for ceremonies.

A longer pigtail, often extended by a hairpiece, appeared from 1750 among the high-ranking officers. Sometimes it hung down to the waist. A silk ribbon was wreathed round the whole length of the pigtail. This was, apart from keeping the hair in place, a precaution against soiling the coat with powder. This pigtail, even when shortened, was never worn by all the troops. Only a few units adopted it very late in the century, particularly in the light infantry.

INFANTRY 1760–70

1. Soldier of the 36th Regiment in uniform during the period of change around 1760 — 2. Fusilier of the 35th Regiment in 1764–5. The carrot-shaped plume is a trophy taken from the French in Canada — 3. Grenadier of the same regiment at the same period. He wears his belt crosswise over the shoulder, a new practice which was soon to become widespread. Note that the first three figures wear smaller leather accessories and cuffs, which were characteristic of this period of change, and also gaiters with leather knee-caps, introduced around 1760 and in general use by 1767. Knee bands, of a type used by the cavalry, were sometimes worn underneath the gaiters with knee-caps in order to protect the breeches against the rubbing of the leather. Breeches, red until then, began to appear in buff or beige towards 1760–1, then from 1767 onwards they were commonly white — 4. Grenadier of the 53rd Regiment in 1768. He wears the new style of fur cap with a metal band. The fur cap of fig. 3 was only a transitional model — in fact it was the old cap of embroidered cloth recovered with fur, sometimes completely, or, in this case, except for the front flap — 5. and 6. Details of styles in 1768. The plaited cord we see at the base of fig. 5 served as a chin-strap to keep the cap in place, but it was worn at the nape of the neck, under the bun of plaited hair — 7. Fusilier of the 7th Regiment in 1770. The cap did not carry the grenade at the back. At least until this date the old embroidered cap was used, in spite of the regulations of 1768 — 8. Corporal of the 25th Regiment in 1770 — 9. Grenadier of the 57th Regiment in 1770 — 10. Corporal of the 11th Regiment in 1770.

1 Page 105, no. 6.

5
6
1
2
3
4
7
8
9
10

Dress-coat and jacket

The illustrations show better than long descriptions the evolution of these essential elements of uniform. Note that the jacket has nine to ten buttonholes depending on the size of the soldier.

The coat had developed slowly until it finally had lapels which showed the jacket off to advantage. Between 1797 and 1800 the dress-coat was to undergo a complete transformation and become 'modern' to the point of outdating those of other nations.

Gaiters

These were white for special occasions, but for marching they were grey, at least since 1744, then black, and sometimes brown from 1749 onwards. New, all-black gaiters appeared in 1760 with leather knee-caps. White gaiters disappeared in 1767. Finally from 1784 they were shortened to knee-length.

Greatcoat

This piece of clothing has rarely been mentioned—at the very most it is referred to for the sentries—but it is obvious that the uniform, even with the buttons done up, would have been inadequate in keeping the troops really warm in very cold weather.

One more often finds references to a covering which was really a blanket worn like a cape. As far as protecting himself against the rain is concerned, the soldier probably had to be patient, get soaked to the skin, and wait until he could dry himself out in the barracks.

INFANTRY 1789–1800

1. Soldier of the 6th Regiment in 1789 — 2. 24th Regiment in 1792 — 3. 5th battalion of light infantry of the 60th or Royal American Regiment in 1797 — 4. 6th battalion of the 60th Regiment in 1799. Several types of foreign flintlocks with rifle barrels were used before the introduction of the Baker Rifle of English make in 1800 — 5. Transitional uniform adopted in May 1797. The coat has the lapels fastened with hooks and eyes over its whole length. They could also be worn turned down and folded over, thus showing the red lining. This uniform certainly did not have time to become widespread for it had to be abandoned in October of the same year — 6. Second transitional uniform, October 1797. The lapels have completely disappeared and the coat is done up with ten buttons. Since the previous year the hat had lost the braid around its border, but it must be noted that some years earlier, after the fashion of the Foot Guards, several regiments (see fig. 1) had anticipated the order. The loop keeping the cockade in place was no longer in distinguishing braid as in figs. 1 and 2, but in white thread; the corners of the hat, on the contrary, were decorated with tassels in white cotton mixed with thread of the distinctive colour. The gaiters, cut under the knee, had been worn since 1784 — 7 and 8. Uniform of 1800. The heavy shako, called the stove-pipe, replaced the hat. The little black cockade had in its centre a regimental button. The plume was red and white for the companies of the centre, white for the grenadiers and dark green for the light company. The little flap fixed to the back of the shako could be turned down when it rained to protect the neck of the soldier against the wet weather. As can be seen, these last two figures offer a striking contrast to the uniforms of the previous year.

1
2
3
4
5
6
7
8

THE PRUSSIAN INFANTRY

Birth of a Kingdom

The first ruler of the Kingdom of Prussia was Frederick I, son of the Grand Elector, Frederick William of Brandenburg.

He came to the throne in 1688 at the age of thirty-one. He refused to accept the will of the dead Electors which divided the territory of Brandenburg between his brothers and himself, but took over all the inherited states with the aim of acquiring the title of King.

In 1701 he obtained the right to change his duchy of Prussia into a kingdom after winning the favour of the Austrian Emperor by helping him in the wars against the Turks and the French. At the same time he accepted a certain suzerainty from Austria in return for backing the Emperor in all questions concerning the Germanic Empire and for maintaining an army of ten thousand men during the whole of the Spanish War of Succession.

Frederick I, an ostentatious king, tried hard to copy the splendours of Louis XIV's court by building luxurious mansions in the baroque style. Although he was an absolute and extravagant king, he supported art, science and literature by founding the Academy of Science in Berlin and instituting the Leibnitz prize.[1]

His son and successor, Frederick William I, a brutal and severe man ended all this luxury and laxity at the court as soon as he came to the throne in 1713.

[1] Gottfried Wilhelm Leibnitz (1646–1716), the famous German philosopher and mathematician.

PRUSSIAN INFANTRY FROM 1701 TO 1740

1. White grenadier of the battalion of the Guard of Frederick I, first king of Prussia from 1701 to 1713—2. Standard-bearer at the time of Frederick I, belonging to the Prince of Orange Regiment (the King's mother was Louise-Henriette of Orange). It was at this time that the Black Eagle of Prussia was replaced by the Red Eagle of Brandenburg—3. Flag at the time of Frederick William I, King of Prussia from 1713 to 1740. Although very similar to both the flags of the last and next reigns (see the pages on flags of the time of Frederick) it does have the anti-Louis XIV motto *Non soli cedit*: It (the Prussian eagle) does not fear the sun (the Sun King). Frederick II, an admirer of France, abolished this motto and replaced it with *Pro gloria et patria*: for glory and the fatherland. The eagle no longer flew 'towards the sun'—4. Officer of the Princes' Regiment circa 1710. He shows the fashion for looking untidy which was very popular at this time. The court of Frederick I was extremely brilliant, extravagant and luxurious. This showy ruler and patron of the arts, transformed Berlin with splendid buildings. The accession of his son, the frugal Frederick William I, put a sudden end to these extravagant frivolities—5. Soldier of the King's Regiment in 1729—6. Grenadier of the 18th or von Gersdorf Regiment in 1730—7. Giant grenadier of the *Rotes Leibbataillion* of the guard of Frederick William I. Recruited throughout Europe, these giants were the pride of this king who was known as the 'Soldier King' in Germany and mocked as the 'Sergeant King' elsewhere. The sovereign's passion for *lange Kerle* (big men) his *liebe blaue Kinder* (children in blue) was such that he had them parade daily, a hundred at a time, past the foot of his bed where he lay waiting to die. He claimed that just a glance at these extraordinary soldiers calmed his suffering. His son and successor, Frederick II, later nicknamed the 'Great' or the 'Unique', abolished this corp to replace it with five new regiments. He was following the advice of his dead father who realised that the upkeep of such a troop, estimated at 300,000 thalers a year, was enough to cover the cost of 10,000 men.

1
2
3
4
5
6
7

As he demanded total obedience from everyone, the new king earned the title of *Herr Despotik*. Miserly, except towards his soldiers, he collected every thaler he could from his subjects, steadily enlarging an already considerable treasury and following his motto *Ein Plus machen* – make a profit. Although nothing of great importance may have happened during his reign, the despotic 'Soldier King', was a good administrator, and taught the Prussians to be active, sober and economical. He abolished slavery and tried to let justice reign. He wanted to rule his people as a father, with a stern and heavy hand to lift his country to the rank of a great power.

On the death of his father (Frederick William I) in 1740, Frederick II was given the name of *Friedrich der Einzige* – Frederick the Unique – but he soon disappointed his subjects who had hoped for a return to the joy and extravagance of the first years of the century. The people were unhappy to see this young man, twenty-eight years old, learned in the arts, science and the philosophies of Plato, Fenelon and the Utopianists, taking control with a firmness and resolution which was unexpected.

Frederick II called himself 'the first servant of the state'. He applied himself to the development and prosperity of his kingdom and to the improvement of the army in preparation for the struggles he was about to have with the other European powers. He earned himself the reputation of being the greatest captain of his time.

PRUSSIAN INFANTRY UNDER FREDERICK THE GREAT I

1ST REGIMENT

At this time the regiments were named after their colonel and this name changed frequently. The first regiment, shown here, changed its name three times between 1756 and 1768 and it was the same for most of the other regiments. However, the record is held by the 9th regiment which changed its name five times in sixteen years. We have therefore adopted the usual practice of the German masters who class the units according to the order of 1806 which gave numbers to the regiments. The reader will, however, find the succession of names of the regiments in the main text.

1. *Musketier*—2. *Idem* in marching order. Notice the typical shoulder strap sewn across the top of the shoulder blade—3. Officer—4. Grenadier—5. Hat showing the way in which one of the two pompoms was attached at the side points—6. and 7. Grenadier's mitre—8. Black and white pompoms of the sergeants—9. Detail of the infantry musket, 1713 to 1722, called the *Henoulgewehr*, manufactured in Liège by F. Henoul who was rewarded in 1713 with the title of 'Grand Armourer of the King of Prussia'. This weapon, very similar to the 1723 model, had a strap with a leather addition which, when attached to the barrel, protected the firing mechanism—10. and 11. Details of the pocket and the back of the coat worn by the 1st regiment. It was the same for all other regiment except that the braiding varied.

PRUSSIA
FLAGS, OFFICERS AND DRUMMERS

(pages 136 and 137)

1. King Frederick II. He is wearing the badge of the Black Eagle, the highest Prussian order, founded by Frederick on the eve of his coronation in 1701—2. The Count von Schwerin, who was killed at Prague in 1757—3. Prince Henri, the King's brother, victor of the Battle of Freiberg in 1767—4. Senior mounted officer of the 16th regiment—5. *Grefrieiter-Korporal* (second corporal) flag bearer of the 1st regiment. Notice the stick hanging from the right lapel. This was worn by all sergeants. The point at the end of the flag staff is not the ferrule, but a copper protective covering—6. Officer of the 12th regiment with spontoon—7. Colonel's flag of the 1st regiment—8. *Kompaniefahne* of the same regiment. It has exactly the same designs as the previous one except that the colours are reversed and the central emblem is on a white background—9. 40th regiment—10. 24th regiment—11. 35th regiment—12. 52nd regiment—13. 27th regiment—14. 16th regiment—15. 11th regiment—16. 31st regiment—17. 1st regiment, called the *Liebgarde* regiment. The last two emblems date back to the reign of Frederick the Great—18. Flag bearer of the 18th regiment—19. Drummer of the 12th regiment—20. Drummer of the 30th regiment—21. Drummer of the 20th regiment. Below: details of the trimmings. This trimming which decorated the sleeves of the coat in particular, was sewn horizontally (fig 20), diagonally (fig 21) or in the form of chevrons (fig 19). This last is the most usual arrangement.

5
6
8
7
10
11
1
2
3
4
9
L. & I. Funcken

7
16
15
14
13
12
11
10
9
18
21
20
19
6

8
7
3
2
5
1
4
L. & F. FUNCKEN

Birth of an Army

At his death on 8 May 1688, Frederick William of Brandenburg left thirteen regiments of infantry and ten of cavalry to his son Frederick III who later became King of Prussia with the title of Frederick I. With a few other garrison troops, these regiments totalled 30,000 men.

Frederick I increased this army by some 5,000 soldiers. His son, Frederick William I, thus inherited a force of 35,000 men in 1713.

His fervent military interest[1] earned Frederick William the nickname of 'Soldier King' or 'Sergeant King' by his enemies. During the last year of his reign, of the seven million thalers he got from taxes, he allocated five million to his army.

On his death, Prussian armed forces totalled 81,034 men, of which 52,391 were foot soldiers.

Frederick II increased the infantry by eighteen regiments before the Seven Years' War broke out. He left an army of 200,000 soldiers including fifty-five infantry regiments, to his successor.

Frederick William II only increased this number to 232,000 men which included three new infantry regiments: the 56th, 57th and 58th. During the reign of Frederick William II, this army experienced a military disaster against Napoleon – the *Katastrophe* of 1806.

[1] Frederick William exchanged his father's precious collection of chinese porcelain for a regiment of Saxon Dragoons.

PRUSSIAN INFANTRY UNDER FREDERICK THE GREAT II

1. 1st regiment (see page 135)—2. 2nd regiment, sergeant and soldier—3. 3rd regiment, officer and soldier—4. 4th regiment, old style officer's coat. It was worn by certain old soldiers until 1776. On the right, a soldier's coat—5. 5th regiment, sergeant and soldier—6. 6th regiment, sergeant and soldier—7. 7th regiment, grenadier's mitre, front and side view and the coat of an ordinary musketeer—8. 8th regiment, grenadier's mitre and trooper's coat—9. 9th regiment, troopers coat, back and front view—10. 10th regiment, trooper's coat and grenadier's mitre—11. 11th regiment, grenadier's mitre and trooper's coat—12. 12th regiment, officer and soldier—13. 13th regiment, officer and soldier—14. 14th regiment, sergeant and soldier—15. 1st battalion of the 15th *Leibgarde* regiment, officer and soldier—15b. Grenadier of the 3rd battalion of the 15th Guard regiment. The 2nd battalion had the same uniform but wore a hat. There existed besides, a corps of *Unrangierten* of the *Ersatzformation der Garde* or training corps which provided replacements. The uniform was identical to that of the 28th regiment of the line but with red collar and cuffs and buttonholes outlined with black piping. The hat had no braiding but a red, white and blue pompom, the red being in the centre—16. 16th regiment, officer and soldier—17. 17th regiment, officer and soldier.

2
3
4
5
6
7
8
9
10
11
12
13
14
15a
15b
16
17

Organization of the Prussian Infantry

At the time of the Seven Years' War, the Prussian Infantry included three kinds of foot soldiers.
(1) The Musketeer or ordinary foot-soldier who wore a tricorne hat.
(2) The Fusiliers or light foot-soldier who were used in the same way as the musketeers but wore a special mitre cap.
(3) The Grenadier or elite foot-soldier.

The uniforms are shown in the illustrations and only a few changes were made by Frederick II to his father's troops.

1. The cravats (*Halsbinden*) were red for the established regiments while black was reserved for the new ones.
2. All the new regiments were *Fusiliere* (Fusiliers) while the established ones were *Musketiere* (musketeers). Besides this, of the old regiments, Nos 29, 30, 31 and 32 changed the mitre cap for the tricorne and so became musketeers.
3. The gaiters, which were white up to the Seven Years' War, were replaced in winter by black ones.
4. The Police hat, was made in the same material as the jacket (but not the coat) with the regimental pompon on the top.
5. The Sergeant's hat was decorated with gold or silver braid. All the embellishments of the coat were in the same metal as the buttons.
6. The officers of the established regiments had a white cravat and a hat with a narrow braid. The officers of the new regiments had a black cravat and a wide braid with a black cockade as well.

Hair

In the reign of the 'Soldier King', hair was tied back in a pigtail. The ducats of 1718 – the *Schwanzdukaten* (pigtail ducats) showed the king wearing his hair in this style.

Under Frederick II the pigtails were grown as far as the waist but under his successors they were shortened to 31.5cm in 1803 and 10.5cm in 1806 (it was not allowed to be longer than to the collar). By 1806 the new recruits wore their hair short and the pigtail was finally abolished in 1807.

Hair was still worn powdered for parades. The parade on 30 March 1812 was the first occasion at which hair was seen un-powdered.

PRUSSIAN INFANTRY UNDER FREDERICK THE GREAT III

THE 18TH AND 19TH REGIMENTS

1. Grenadier of the 18th regiment—2. *Idem*, back view. He is wearing the full campaign kit, with the tent pegs, the bread basket, called the *Brotbeutel*, containing 6 pounds of bread, under the kit bag. The heavy cartridge box contained 60 cartridges. The tool has been omitted to give a clearer view of the cartridge box. Notice the decoration, peculiar to the grenadiers. Note also the strap covering the lock of the musket (see detail on the illustration of the 1st regiment)—3. Musketeer of the 19th regiment—4. *Idem*, back view, with full campaign equipment. To visualize the musketeer of the 18th regiment (not depicted here), it is necessary to substitute the colours of the grenadier in figs 1 and 2, that is, the shoulder strap, collar, lapels, cuffs and facings, for those in 3 and 4 and add the hat and the cartridge box of the musketeer—5. Officer of the 18th regiment—6. Officer of the 19th regiment. The officers normally wore beige gauntlet gloves, omitted here in order to show the details of the cuffs. Notice that the officers and men of the 19th regiment wore straw coloured jacket and breeches—7. Detail of the cuff and the sword knot of the 19th regiment. There is an extraordinary likeness, reflecting the scrupulous respect for military traditions, between this eighteenth-century sword knot and those of the twentieth century still used in Germany during the two world wars. (See in the same series *Arms and Uniforms – the First World War* and *Arms and Uniforms – the Second World War*.)

1
2
3
4
5
6
7
L. & F. FUNCKEN

Tactics

The Prussians were the first to exploit the tactics made possible by the flint-lock musket. The rate of firing was increased to three shots a minute by the adoption of the iron ramrod.

Careful research and the ingenious minds of the gunsmiths resulted in the development of stronger and very much better weapons. Improved design and intensive training enabled the Prussian soldiers to produce a phenomenal rate of fire for that time. Voltaire wrote on this subject 'I agree with you that the Prussian King is near-sighted, but he has a most important advantage in the game he is playing – speed. The body of this army has been well trained for forty years. Imagine how regular, hardened robots must react on the battlefield having seen their leader every-day, being known to him and encouraged by him to do their duty. How amusing they seem, doing the side step and quick march and juggling with their cartridges, but do not forget that they fire six or seven rounds a minute.'[1]

In 1720 the Prussian army had adopted the famous thin formation, with successive fire from foot soldiers arranged in three rows and the tight or shoulder to shoulder formation which increased the density of the fire.

The skill of the troops in the use of the musket was the result of hard training devised by Leopold von Dessau who was recognized as the best instructor of the period. Frederick the Great saw the way in which this training could best be used. While other European armies were still using salvo firing in tight formation and volleys in thin formation Frederick II successfully[2] experimented with his revolutionary oblique formation, engaging the enemy face to face then surprising him on the flanks with a strengthened wing.

He must be given credit for teaching patience and determination to an army which, though superb, had only 'made war' on the public squares of Berlin. He himself was new to the game and he learned a great deal while training his army.

His most famous victory at Leuthen[3] on 5 December 1757 inspired Napoleon to describe it as 'A masterpiece of movement, manoeuvres and determination, the battle of Leuthen would in itself be enough to immortalize Frederick and rank him amongst the greatest generals'.

Certainly 'Old Fritz' was no longer the calm philosopher of 1739, the fervent idealist, the intuitive composer and exponent of twenty-five sonatas and four concertos for the flute. Having become a cynical realist he declared 'You take when you can; you are never wrong when you are not obliged to give in.'

Disappointing though this change may seem, Frederick, a frail, stooping man who revealed an inflexible will in his haughty, piercing glance, remained basically a simple man without the boastful manner so typical of other historical heroes. He was distinguished from contemporary monarchs by his one real strength, his intellect.

'If he had not been a King or a General, he would have been one of the most important men of his century' affirms Michelet.[4]

[1] Letter addressed to M. d'Argens from Lausanne on 8 January 1758.

[2] Except at Kolin (Czechoslovakia) on 18 June 1757 when the Austrian enemy did not maintain the passive attitude necessary for the success of this tactic.

[3] Now Lutynia in Poland, west of Wroclaw. The site of a victory against the Austrians.

[4] Jules Michelet (1798–1874). Seen in its true light, the judgement of this historian, whose works seem sometimes too monumental, is more fully researched than one would think.

PRUSSIAN INFANTRY UNDER FREDERICK THE GREAT IV

20. to 35. The 20th to 35th regiments. The officer's uniforms are on the left and those of the soldiers on the right. Notice the special headgear of the 33rd to 35th regiments in the form of a badly shaped mitre. Being fusiliers, these men did not wear the usual type of headgear.

20
21
22
23
24
25
26
27
28
29
30
31
32
33
34
35

A Great Master of Uniform

The German painter and designer Adolf Friedrich Erdmann von Menzel must be mentioned in any study of the uniforms of Frederick's reign. He treated them with the skill and precision of a master.

Born in Breslau on 8 December 1815, Menzel was an extremely small man. From the age of fifteen he had to give way to the needs of his mother and four sisters by working as a lithographer in the tiny family printing house in Berlin.

His first drawings illustrating a Goethe poem were noticed by the historian Franz Kugler who was preparing a *Life of Frederick the Great* for publication. The young, unknown artist was asked to tackle the four hundred illustrations required, an undertaking which was to determine his future career.

Completed in 1842, this work inspired Menzel to continue his research into the armies of the great King. He first published *The Review of Frederick the Great's Soldiers* with 32 plates and then *The Army of Frederick the Great* produced in chromolithography between 1842 and 1857. Only thirty copies were published. The three volumes of this rare work are today enormously expensive and the 1906 edition in facsimile is extremely rare.[1]

Adolf von Menzel produced many paintings for the Emperor William II of Germany, affectionately called the *Kleine Excellenz* (Little Excellency). This artist, who was literally covered with honours, died in Berlin on 9 February 1905.

[1] The reader will find it easier to consult the admirable book by Dr Hans Bleekwenn *Die Uniformen der Infanterie, 1753–1786*, illustrated with 144 colour plates by Fritz Gunther Melzner (Biblio Verlag, Osnabrück).

Frederick the Great's Infantry

The regiments of Frederick the Great usually bore the name of their Colonel though, for reasons of simplication they are numbered in the illustrations according to the order of 1806. Although this system of identification was more evocative than a number, the name changed with every new commander. The following list gives some indication of the various names of the regiments.

At the time of the Seven Years' War (1756 to 1763):

1. Winterfeldt (1756); Lattorff (1758); Zeuner (1760).
2. Kanitz (1750).
3. Anhalt-Dessau, Leopold Friedrich Franz Prince of (1752); Kahlden (1758); Anhalt-Bernburg-Schaumburg, Franz Adolph Prince of (1759).
4. Kalnein (1745); Rautter (1757); Kleist (1758); Thadden (1761).
5. Brunswick, Ferdinand Duke of (Alt-Braunschweig) (1756).
6. Grenadier Guard Battalion (former Riesengarde), from 1743 on named after their commander. Retzow (1745); Saldern (1760).
7. Braunschweig-Lüneburg-Bevern, August Wilhelm Duke of (1741) (1757 Alt-Bevern).
8. Amstel (1754); Hagen or Geist (1757); Queiss (1759).

PRUSSIAN INFANTRY UNDER FREDERICK THE GREAT V

36TH AND 37TH REGIMENTS

1. Fusilier of the 36th regiment. On the left is the shoulder strap—2. Officer of the 36th regiment—3. Drummer of the 36th regiment. Notice the details of the braid (on the right). Its position around the buttons at the waist was peculiar to the drummer—4. Fusilier of the 37th regiment. On the left is the shoulder strap—5. Officer of the 37th regiment—6. Fusilier of the 37th regiment in fatigue dress with the police cap in the regimental colour. On the right is the shoulder strap.

1
2
3
4
5
6

9. Quadt von Wickradt (1747); Kleist (1756) (Jung-Kleist); Oldenburg (1758); Puttkamer (1758); Schenckendorff (1759); (from 1760 Jung-Schenckendorff).
10. Knobloch (1750); Pannwitz (1757); Mosel (1759).
11. Below (1749); Rebentisch (1758).
12. Hessen-Darmstadt, Ludwig Hereditary Prince of (1743) (until 1747 Alt-Darmstadt); Finck (1757).
13. Itzenplitz (1750); Syburg (1760); Peter III, Tsar of Russia (1762); Wylich and Lottum (1763).
14. Lehwaldt (1738).
15. Garde (from 1.6.1740).
16. Dohna (1748); Syburg (1762).
17. Jeetze (1748) (until 1752 Jung-Jeetze); Manteuffel (1756).
18. Prince of Prussia (1744).
19. Brandenburg, Karl Albrecht Margrave of (1731). Tettenborn (1762).
20. Borcke (1746) (until 1747 Jung-Borcke); Zastrow (1756); Bornstedt (1757); Stutterheim (1759); (Jung-Stutterheim).
21. Bredow (1744); Hülsen (1756).
22. Anhalt-Dessau, Moritz Prince of (1741); Schenckendorff (1760); (Alt-Schenckendorff until 1763; The description 'Prince Moritz' is still used also).
23. Forcade de Biaix (1748).
24. Schwerin (1723); Goltz (1757); vacant 1761–1763; Diringshofen (1763).
25. Kalckstein (1729); Ramin (1760).
26. Meyerinck (1749); Wedell (1758); Linden (1760).
27. Kleist (1747) (until 1749 Jung-Kleist); Asseburg (1757); Rindstedt (1759).
28. Herault de Hautcharmoy (1742); Münchow (1758) (Jung-Münchow); Kreytzen (1758) (Jung-Kreytzen); Ramin (1759); Thile (1760).
29. Schultze (1747); Wedell (1758); Knobloch (1758).
30. Blanckensee (1755); Pritz (1756); Kannacher (1757); Stutterheim (1759) (Alt-Stutterheim).
31. Lestwitz (1746).
32. Treskow (1747) (until 1754 Jung-Treskow).
33. La Motte-Fouqué (1744).
34. Prussia, Ferdinand Prince of (1740).
35. Prussia, Heinrich Prince of (1740).
36. Münchow (1740) (1758 Alt-Münchow).
37. Kurssell (1755); Braun (1758).
38. Brandes (1749); Zastrow (1758).
39. Braunschweig-Lüneburg-Wolfenbüttel, Friedrich Franz Prince of (1745) (from 1755 Jung-Braunschweig). 1758–1763 vacant, but thereafter called Jung-Braunschweig.
40. Kreytzen (1750) (from 1758 Alt-Kreytzen); Gabelentz (1759).
41. Wied zu Neuwied (1746).
42. Brandenburg-Schwedt, Heinrich Friedrich Margrave of (1741).
43. Kalsow (1744); Kalckreuth (1757); Bredow (1758); Zieten (1760); (Jung-Zieten).
44. Jungkenn called Müntzer von Mohrenstamm (1749); Hoffmann (1759); Grant (1760).
45. Dossow (1743); Hessen-Kassel, Friedrich II Landgrave of (1757).
46. Württemberg, Karl Eugen Duke of (1743) (Alt-Württemberg); Bülow (1757).
47. Wietersheim (1752); Rohr (1756); Grabow (1758).
48. Hessen-Kassel, Friedrich II Landgrave of (1756); Salmuth called Beringer (1757); Beckwith (1763).
49. Pionniers von Sers (1748). From 1758 Fusilier-Regiment Diericke (1758).

Regiments created 1772–1774

50. Rossières (1773).
51. Laxdehnen (1773).
52. Lengefeld (1772).
53. Luck (1773).
54. Rohr (1773).
55. Hessen-Philippsthal, Adolph Prince of (1774).

PRUSSIAN INFANTRY UNDER
FREDERICK THE GREAT VI

38. to 53. 38th to 53rd regiments. Officers' uniforms on the left and soldiers' on the right. With the exception of the 50th or von Rossières battalion, all these regiments were made up of fusiliers as can be seen from the soldier's hats. However, it must be remembered that these regiments had a company of grenadiers whose men wore the traditional mitre of these elite troops but still used the regimental colour and characteristic metal of the spurious mitre of the regiment to which they were attached.

38
39
40
41
42
43
44
45
46
47
48
49
50
51
52
53

The Garrison Regiments

On the death of Frederick the Great, the Prussian army was composed of the regiments listed above, of which the first thirty-two were made up of musketeers and grenadiers, while the 33rd to 35th were made up of fusiliers. The battalion of light infantry, *Jägerkorps zu Fuss*, and the twelve regiments of garrison troops, *the Garnisonsregimenter*, must not be forgotten. These garrison troops guarded strongholds but were frequently used for other less static war-like pursuits, depending on the circumstances.

Frederick II had, over the years, tripled the first four garrison regiments which existed at the beginning of his reign. Their uniform was exactly the same as that of the regiments of the line but in the simplest of styles, without lapels or decorations of any sort. The coat, jacket and breeches were all dark blue. Details are given in the table on page 150.

The officers' uniform was characterized by the long tails without facings and by a narrow gold or silver braid around the edge of the hat. The soldier had tails turned back to show the lining which was red for all regiments. The sergeants wore the big black and white pompom of their rank, and also, in the 9th, 10th and 12th regiments, a braid matching the metal of the buttons.

All the soldiers wore the black cravat (*Halsbinde*) around their necks. Each regiment had its grenadiers with their own particular hat, the mitre. Its front arch-shaped piece was richly decorated and stamped with metal leaf to match the regimental buttons.

The garrison troops were abolished in 1788 and were absorbed into the new fusilier regiments and the remainder of the old regiments of the line.

PRUSSIAN INFANTRY UNDER FREDERICK THE GREAT VII

54TH AND 55TH REGIMENTS

1. Fusilier of the 54th regiment. He is tearing the cartridge paper which contains the powder and the bullet. Notice the 'Swedish' cuffs which are open underneath—2. Grenadier of the 54th regiment. He is pulling out the ramrod which will ram home the bullet and the powder charge in the breech of the musket barrel—3. Officer of the 54th regiment—4. Officer of the 55th regiment—5. Fusilier of the 55th regiment. On the left, his shoulder strap—6. Grenadier of the 55th regiment. After firing, the order *Schulter's Gewehr!* (Shoulder arms) was given. The soldier is depicted here in the required position.

Details of the cuffs (the right sleeve is given here): 7. Swedish —8. Brandenburg—9. Straight, with the extra braiding reserved for the sergeants—10. Details of the sergeant's halberd. For the fusiliers, it measured 2.10m, 3m for the musketeers and 3.80m for the grenadiers. The staff was always of a beautiful reddish-brown colour and varnished.

1
2
3
4
5
6
7
8
9
10

NAME OF REGIMENT	COLLAR	CUFFS-COLOUR AND TYPE	BUTTONS	POMPOM	POMPOM ON THE POINTS OF THE HAT
1. Luck	—	Basic [a]	silver	red	bright green
2. Sydow	—	White [b]	silver	grey	white
3. Hellermann	Red	basic	gold	sky blue	red
4. Grape	—	basic	gold	white with red centre	white with red centre
5. Sydow	—	black	gold	white with grey centre	white
6. Lattorf	—	pink	silver	white with red circle in centre	white with red centre
7. Lange	—	crimson	gold	white	white
8. Knobelsdorf	—	black [b]	gold	sky blue	sky blue
9. La Motte	Black	black [b]	gold	blue with yellow centre	yellow
10. Blanckensee	—	black [b]	silver	red	red
11. Manteuffel	—	crimson	silver	yellow	red
12. Kalckreuth	—	black [b]	gold	red	red

(a) The colour of the coat was light blue.

(b) Swedish. All the other cuffs were the straight type, also called round cuffs. The different styles are shown in the illustrations depicting the 54th and 55th regiments on page 149.

The Light Infantry and the Free Corps

The Light Infantry

The first corps of the light infantry were formed by Frederick II shortly after his accession in 1744.

The coat and jacket of this newly formed *Jägerkorps zu Fuss* (corps of light infantry) were made in canary green cloth. The cartridge case in brown leather was worn across the stomach, as shown in the illustration. This was a new addition to the regular troops of the King of Prussia.

From 1744 to 1760 black gaiters were worn, but these were then replaced by some really odd-looking cavalry boots.

PRUSSIA, THE LIGHT INFANTRY AND THE FREE CORPS

1. Light infantry corps of foot soldiers. This corps was part of the regular infantry, in contrast with the others shown here—2. Light infantryman of the Fransciscus Le Noble battalion formed in 1756 and abolished in 1763. Notice the short muskets of these two figures—3. Musketeer of the Franciscus Le Noble battalion, 1756 to 1763—4. Drummer of the Count Johann Ludwig von Hordt regiment, formed in 1758 and disbanded in 1762. His cuffs are of the 'straight' or 'rounded' variety with a braided edge. On the sleeve two little button-holes closed the split as in fig 8 of the preceding page—5. Officer of the von Wunsch battalion formed in 1758—6. Officer of the von Wunsch regiment, formed in 1759—7. Musketeer of the Karl Gottlieb Guichard regiment, called 'Quintus Icillius' in 1760—8. Grenadier of the Major Heer regiment in 1760—9. Grenadier of the Major von Schony regiment, disbanded in 1763. Note the fur caps which were unusual for Prussian troops, but were worn by troops formed from deserters from the Austrian Imperial Army.

2
5
6
7
8
9
4
3
1
L. & F. Funcken

The Free Corps

These troops, formed at the outbreak of the Seven Years' War and given the name of *Freikorps*, never attained the level of efficiency of the regiments of the line. They seem to have been regarded as reservists and were not thought capable of serving in battle and were relegated to guard duties.

Nevertheless, on at least one occasion, under the command of Prince Henry of Prussia, the King's brother, the Free Corps contributed to a victory. This was at the battle of Freiberg[1] against the Austrians in 1762, along with regiments of the line and garrison troops. The most famous of these corps, and one of the largest, was the *Freikorps von Kleist* which included infantry, light infantry, dragoons and hussars.

Other, much weaker, units were often raised only for a period of a few months.

The uniform most often worn was distinguished by its bright blue jacket and breeches. This colour was also used for the cuffs and lapels of the dark blue coat. Some of these troops were also attached to the established regiments, in which case they wore a bright green coat and cavalry boots. The hat was sometimes the tricorne but a sort of mitre cap was also worn. This mitre cap, made of dressed leather had the royal cipher painted on the front.

There was an obvious desire to look like regular troops. However, the result was a confusion of uniforms amongst which one could notice the fur-bedecked mitres of the Austrian Army deserters.

[1] A town in East Germany between Dresden and the present Karl-Marx-Stadt (Chemnitz).

PRUSSIA AT THE END OF THE EIGHTEENTH CENTURY

(the reigns of Frederick William II and Frederick William III)

1. Musketeer of the 25th regiment in 1790—2. Fusilier of a light infantry regiment circa 1790. At first, green jackets and breeches were worn—3. Grenadier of the 6th regiment in 1786. Later, the fine mitre was changed for a hat called a *Kasket*—4. Grenadier wearing the *Kasket* in 1790—5. Grenadier of a regiment of the line in 1799 with the new mitre adopted by the Guards in 1798. The front part was made of leather decorated with copper. The hat was made of felt with a central band in the regimental colour. This mitre has often been depicted as being taller, but in fact, the front part measured only 26cm—6. Officer of the light infantry in 1790—7. Flag of the 56th regiment (Ansbach Bayreuth) in 1795—8. Flag of the 57th regiment in 1798—9. Detail of the badge in fig 1 (Friedrich Wilhelm Rex)—10. Detail of the eagle on the band of the mitre in fig 5—11. Detail of emblem of the fusiliers (fig 2).

Note the falling off in the bearing of fig 4 in comparison with figs 3 and 5. The uniform is hardly more attractive despite the new mitre cap and this rather unmilitary hat had a bad effect on the morale of an army. There seems to have been psychological problems with the hat which perhaps contributed to the catastrophic defeats of the beginning of the next century.

L. & F. Funcken
7
8
1
2
3
4
5
6
9
10
11

The Successors of Frederick the Great

On the death of Frederick II in 1786, his heir presumptive and nephew Frederick William II came to the throne. The poor opinion which the great king had of his future successor had been somewhat altered by the bravery shown by the prince during the war of Bavarian Succession in 1778.

Frederick William undertook, in 1795, ruinous offensives against revolutionary France when he sent 45,000 soldiers to sink into the marshes of Champagne. He also participated in the second and third Partitions of unfortunate Poland, thus going against his word of honour.[1]

Prussia gained 2,200,000 inhabitants by this act and yet another 85,000 through the annexation of the principalities of Ansbach and Bayreuth. These were later formally purchased. However, at the end of his reign, the public treasury was empty of the seven million crowns left by Frederick II.

However, the positive aspects of his reign must not be forgotten; the foundation of educational institutions, the publication of Prussian law and the reduction of public taxes. An enthusiastic violinist himself, the king founded the Academy of Music where he welcomed Mozart and Beethoven who dedicated several pieces of music to him. He also patronized the growth of the theatre and architecture.[2]

In the area of uniforms, Frederick William II seems to have been bent on disfiguring the marvellous army which he had inherited. He introduced the bicorne, called the *Kasket*. Its brim could be pulled down over the eyes or the neck, but it was unattractive and unpopular and though inexpensive its adoption was certainly not justified by the raising of three poor regiments.

Frederick William III succeeded Frederick William II in 1797 but he never mastered an inferiority complex contracted during an unhappy childhood. He did his best however to correct the errors made by his father and he was very ably backed by his wife, Luise von Mecklenburg-Strelitz (1776–1810). Loved by the people for her charm and patriotism, later this queen was to become the heart of the resistance to Napoleon I.

The young king's policy of neutrality during the second and third coalition[3] against France altered the military prestige of Prussia and led it to the humiliation which followed the crushing defeat of Iena in 1806.

The old tricorne, or at least a headdress that closely resembled it, was once more introduced at this time. A new-style mitre gave back a little prestige to the grenadiers who greeted it with enthusiasm. The men boasted of its originality, its beauty, its utility, so superior to the old mitre which reminded one of a Chinese hat!

[1] The King was committed by the Treaty of 1790 to support Poniatowski, the succession to the throne and the integrity of the Kingdom of Poland to which he had to provide a force of 40,000 foot soldiers and 4,000 cavalrymen in case of attack by any power.

[2] The famous Brandenburg Gate was built in his reign.

[3] The second coalition (1779–1802) united Austria, Russia, England, Turkey and the two Sicilies against Republican France. It was broken by the French victories at Zurich, Marengo and Hohenlinden. The third coalition in 1805 grouped Austria, Russia and England against Napoleonic France and was broken after Ulm and Austerlitz.

Index

The page numbers in italic refer to the illustrations